the *Ultimate* Soup CLEANSE

the Ultimate Soup

CLEANSE

60 Recipes to Reduce, Restore, Renew & Resolve

NICOLE PISANI AND KATE ADAMS

authors of
Magic Soup: 100 Recipes for Health and Happiness

ATRIA BOOKS

NEW YORK   LONDON   TORONTO   SYDNEY   NEW DELHI

ATRIA BOOKS

An Imprint of Simon & Schuster, Inc.
1230 Avenue of the Americas
New York, NY 10020

First Atria Books hardcover edition December 2016

ATRIA BOOKS and colophon are trademarks of Simon & Schuster, Inc.

For information about special discounts for bulk purchases, please contact Simon & Schuster Special Sales at 1-866-506-1949 or business@simonandschuster.com.

The Simon & Schuster Speakers Bureau can bring authors to your live event. For more information or to book an event contact the Simon & Schuster Speakers Bureau at 1-866-248-3049 or visit our website at www.simonspeakers.com.

Photography by Regula Ysewijn

Interior design by Amy Trombat

Manufactured in the United States of America

10 9 8 7 6 5 4 3 2 1

Library of Congress Cataloging-in-Publication Data

Names: Pisani, Nicole, author. | Adams, Kate (Health publisher), author.
Title: The ultimate soup cleanse / Nicole Pisani and Kate Adams, authors of Magic Soup: 100 recipes for Health and Happiness.
Description: First Atria hardcover edition. | New York : Atria Paperback, 2016.
Identifiers: LCCN 2016021636 (print) | LCCN 2016022894 (ebook) | ISBN 9781501145940 (hardback) | ISBN 9781501145964 (eBook)
Subjects: LCSH: Soups. | Soups—Health aspects. | Detoxification (Health) | BISAC: COOKING / Courses & Dishes / Soups & Stews. | COOKING / Health & Healing / Weight Control. | COOKING / Specific Ingredients / Natural Foods. | LCGFT: Cookbooks.
Classification: LCC TX757 .P573 2015 (print) | LCC TX757 (ebook) | DDC 641.81/3—dc23
LC record available at https://lccn.loc.gov/2016021636

ISBN 978-1-5011-4594-0
ISBN 978-1-5011-4596-4 (ebook)

Contents

Introduction

We'll be honest: however much we would like to be those people who treat their bodies as temples for 365 days of the year, the truth is that every now and then we need to balance out the inevitable indulgences with a few days of saintliness. The signs become clear: our pants feel tight, but somehow we always seem to feel hungry, wanting to bite into every cake or pastry that we see.

Our bodies get used to eating and wanting more too quickly. Why it doesn't happen the other way around seems to us to be one of life's little cruel ironies. But if we can gather our collective willpower and fill our cupboards with delicious ingredients for making quick-and-easy healthy recipes that we actually enjoy eating, then we give ourselves the best chance for getting off to a fresh start.

While working hard for five years to keep off the 35 pounds she lost, Kate finds that it is much easier to do so when she focuses on the things she *can* eat rather than worrying about all the things she can't. We don't think extreme deprivation works; we believe that *nourishing* works, which is why in this book you'll discover appetizing, healthy, happy soups that will become your favorites. For us, food is always an adventure and should also be a source of enjoyment.

Treat yourself to *The Ultimate Soup Cleanse* to reset your inner and outer balance. Feel good, eat well, and:

- Lose weight
- Wake up with energy
- Feel less bloated
- Get a better night's sleep
- Have less stress
- Feel more clearheaded
- Fall back in love with your body

Our philosophy is simple: eat a wide variety of natural, healthful, and seasonal foods, and cook them all from scratch. Eating and living this way even feels indulgent and like a treat, especially when we take the time to shop for interesting ingredients, plan recipes, and enjoy every mouthful. We become more aware of our taste buds and how we're feeling. We try our best to think before we eat, look for ways to be more active, and take the stress and overcomplication out of our lives.

Take this approach step by step. Make one small change at a time and use that as a catalyst to make other tweaks and improvements in your life. We kid ourselves that there are people out there who are somehow perfect in every way—they never eat chocolate, they do meditation and yoga every morning before the rest of us are even awake. Perfection is highly overrated, because in reality it's impossible to achieve, and living that way would be boring. We are all imperfect, but wonderful as we are.

"Great things are not done by impulse, but by a series of small things brought together."

VINCENT VAN GOGH

It's tempting to think that we need to completely overhaul our lifestyles, to become the "new me" and put aside all the positive things that we already do in our lives. We are great believers that one change can lead to another, and that we can feel good all the way along the journey. Even when it comes to eating a little less or making healthier food choices, we need to get used to how different our bodies feel when we're not grabbing food throughout the day, but instead make conscious choices about what we eat. There's a Buddhist saying about never feeling that small good deeds don't make a difference, but that a jug fills "drop by drop."

As a result, *The Ultimate Soup Cleanse* is designed so you can start with a 2-day cleanse over a weekend, or one of the 5- or 7-day cleanses if you're willing to commit to a longer period of time. We hope that the recipes offer inspiration as much as guidance and that they become a catalyst for falling in love with the healthy side of you, the one that might even like kale and tofu (we promise!).

1. RESOLVE

2-day ultimate cleanse to resolve any excess water retention and give your body a break from any foods that may be inflammatory

2. REBALANCE

7-day weight-loss cleanse

3. RESTORE

7-day restoring and strengthening digestion

4. RENEW

5-day nutrient-rich energizing cleanse

Why Cleanse?

For us, a cleanse is a way to bring ourselves back into balance. You know the feeling you get when you have been overindulging for too long, or you wish you could get up in the morning with a little more spring in your step and feeling more energized? Or when you know your digestive system is struggling—you might feel bloated or sluggish, or perhaps intolerant to foods that you can enjoy with no problems when you're on vacation.

When we're willing to listen, our bodies give us the signs we need to know that a few days of simple eating and simple living are a good idea. In today's fast-paced world, it's not always easy to slow down; many of us tend to get away with constantly running on empty, with the occasional vacation here and there to top off our reserves. Taking the time to restore, replenish, and look after your body feels like a luxury, but when you do give yourself this gift, the benefits will last.

Signs that you might benefit from a cleanse:

- Decreased energy
- Feeling tired after eating
- Suffering from constipation, loose stools, or irregular bowel movements

- Having a foggy brain
- Having trouble sleeping or finding it hard to wake up
- Feeling anxious or stressed
- Craving specific foods or feeling a dependence on certain foods
- Feeling bloated
- Experiencing weight gain
- Feeling generally "off" your game

A cleanse aims for:

- A renewed sense of vitality and clarity
- Supporting a sustained healthy weight
- Promoting deep and restorative sleep
- Regular, healthy bowel movements
- Energy throughout the day
- A positive, balanced relationship with food
- Feeling revitalized and enthusiastic about life

Why Go on a Soup Cleanse?

"The transformation that occurs in the cauldron is quintessential and wondrous, subtle and delicate."

I YIN (239 BC)

Soup came into being about five millennia ago when humans began to farm and cultivate food in addition to hunting and gathering it; this marked a crucial stage in human development. When people began to put different ingredients into a pot with water over the heat of the fire, they created broths and stews. The discovery of boiling and simmering foods together meant that a much greater variety of plants and grains could be combined and eaten. Meat provided even more nutrition when the bones were boiled.

These bone broths became the basis of the first restaurants, which appeared in Paris in the eighteenth century. Their name came from the fact that they served *restaurants*, which were usually meat consommés or bouillons that would help "restore" a person's strength and vitality—or cure a hangover. Bone-based broths have been used across cultures for centuries as healing remedies. Soup has long been a healing centerpiece used by various traditional medicines. In Ayurveda, a soup (kitchari) cleanse is undertaken to help restore digestive "fire," which is not only related to how our body digests the food we eat but also to all our thoughts and emotions. Supporting the health of this fire, or *agni*, is a way of supporting our overall health.

In Chinese medicine, it has been thought for thousands of years that consuming a bowl of soup before each meal is beneficial to one's health. Contemporary research suggests that this practice leads to eating fewer calories over the course of the day.

So soups are not just restorative, they're also a great choice if you want to lose weight healthily. In fact, when it comes to eating well, variety has been shown to be a crucial factor for making positive long-term changes and choices. We enjoy a food trend as much as anyone—our cupboards and refrigerator are filled with coconut oil, kale, and various seeds—but we also love the simplicity and the purpose of soup. It *is* restoring; it is clean *and* comforting. It also turns out that soup has even more than the test of time on its side when it comes to weight-loss benefits.

Soup has been shown by researchers to keep us fuller for longer per calorie compared when eating the same ingredients in a "dry" dish, like a salad. This is because soup takes up more room in the stomach, which turns off ghrelin, the appetite or "hunger" hormone, quicker than a salad does. Specific cells in the stomach wall release ghrelin when the stomach is empty. Ghrelin then travels via the bloodstream to the brain's appetite center, the hypothalamus, and tells you that you are hungry. When your stomach is full, ghrelin is no longer released and so the appetite signal is turned off. Soup takes more time to leave the stomach, which is why you stay satisfied for longer.

Why cooking is good for you

When you cook from scratch, you tend to eat more natural foods that have undergone less processing. You also know exactly what you are putting into your body. You become more aware of how certain foods make you feel. Despite scientists' best efforts, there really is no one-size-fits-all approach when it comes to knowing which diet is best for everyone. Some people have no problem digesting dairy products, for example, while others have an adverse reaction to milk or butter. Wheat isn't the evil enemy it's made out to be for all of us. For some people, it's the industrial, processed ingredients that cause bloating or a stomachache. When we bake our own bread, using locally grown and milled flours from grains other than just wheat, we discover that we don't have to go through life without bread or pastries.

A key to keeping up healthy habits beyond just a few days is to be adventurous and explore new foods and ways of cooking. Nicole has recently become obsessed with sea spaghetti (seaweed shaped like spaghetti). She uses it alongside noodles, in salads, combined with lentils—and more. It just so happens to be mineral rich and wonderfully good for you, too.

The art of preparing food to take care of your inner temple is soul replenishing. Feeling good about treating yourself well, to present your food to yourself with those little touches like a sprinkle of toasted nuts and seeds or a drizzle of herb-infused oil, makes the cleanse a gift rather than a sacrifice. Take time out of your day to sit down to eat, and be mindful of what you are eating and how you are feeling. This will help you enjoy the journey as much as the end result.

Eat natural

Bircher muesli, a mixture of grains, dried fruit, nuts, and seeds, gets its name from Dr. Maximilian Bircher-Benner, who was a Swiss physician and pioneer in nutritional research. In 1904, Dr. Bircher-Benner set up a sanatorium called Vital Force, based on the German lifestyle reform movement that espouses the idea of living in harmony with nature. Instead of the standard diet of meat and potatoes, Bircher-Benner recommended eating more fruit, vegetables, and nuts.

The more we can live with an awareness of nature, the better it is for our bodies, too. This is what the healthiest cultures in the world have been doing for thousands of years. The Mediterranean diet is based on what's available and grown in the region—olive oil, fish, grains, and vegetables. For the people of Japan, it's fish, rice, and seaweed. A Korean meal wouldn't be complete without kimchi, a traditional condiment made from fermented vegetables and spices.

The people of these cultures eat what is naturally available to them. We feel just as passionate about all the amazing foods grown in our own countries—for Kate that's the United Kingdom and for Nicole it's the island of Malta. In the United Kingdom, berries, game, fish, wild mushrooms, nuts, and herbs have been consumed for centuries. Malta is an island of sunshine, a land with an abundance of ripe tomatoes, figs, olives, fish, and local sourdough bread. We have an abundance of foods available to us year round, and as soon as you tap into choosing as many unprocessed foods as possible, you begin to notice and experience the vibrancy and vitality of these foods.

Eat with the seasons

Nature has a way of providing us with foods that are especially good for us at certain times of the year. During the autumn and winter months, there are plenty of ingredients that are perfect for warming soups and stews: carrots, squash, sweet potatoes, parsnips. In spring,

5

nutrient-rich leafy greens are found in abundance, and in summer, when we need cooling foods, there are cucumbers and lettuces. If you eat what is seasonally available in your own region and climate, you will naturally eat much of what your body needs and wants at a particular time of year.

Autumn and Winter Cleansing

Autumn and winter are not times when the body instinctively wants to cleanse, but with so many of us enjoying the holiday season and all the treats that come with it, it is a time when we need to balance out our overindulgences. We tend to feel hungrier in cold weather to keep warm and take care of our immune systems, so going on a 100% raw-food diet at this time might be a little more than our already strained digestive system can handle. This is why eating soup is such a great way to cleanse; it's the ideal solution for eating a little less, eating natural ingredients, and eating foods that nourish our digestion back to optimum function.

Tips for your autumn or winter cleanse:

- Keep warm. Take baths and wear layers of natural cotton or wool clothing and thick socks or slippers in the evening.
- Stick to warming foods like soups rather than cold juices. If you enjoy a raw salad, balance it with a warm soup first or eat some fermented vegetables such as kimchi (page 67) or sauerkraut.
- Drink plenty of herbal teas.
- Create a vision board for the new year (page 10).

Spring and Summer Cleansing

We don't think it's a coincidence that spring is a time of deep cleaning on all fronts—from the house to our diets to life in general. During the winter, we need to conserve our energy, while in spring that energy can be harnessed and put into action as the days become a little warmer and longer and signs of life appear all around us in nature. Many of the green shoots—such as nettle tops, dandelion greens, and pea shoots—that begin to grow during spring are ideal ingredients for clean eating. Summer means long days and an endless harvest of all kinds of fruits and vegetables.

Tips for spring and summer cleansing:

- Think green in the spring and add vibrant greens to your meals wherever possible.
- If your digestion feels strong, add raw garnishes to your soups, such as sprouted seeds, grated carrots, and shaved fennel.
- Get outside as much as you can to take advantage of the increasing levels of natural light.
- Sow seeds in your garden, a window box, or windowsill pots to harvest later in the season.
- On warm or hot days, eat lighter choices and chilled soups.

Quite often, when we think of healthy eating, we think of having to cut out all the things we like and to try our best to stay on a diet for as long as possible before desperation or boredom gets the better of us. We hope that the ideas and recipes within these pages will prove to you that healthy food can make you feel good and inspired. This is the key to a happy, healthy relationship with what we eat and how we feel about ourselves and our bodies. Love food, love your body.

Mind and body working together

"Tell me what you eat, and I will tell you who you are."

JEAN ANTHELME BRILLAT-SAVARIN

We need to be willing to listen and sometimes talk to ourselves when we are on the road to making healthier choices. Our bodies and minds aren't always in unison. With so many prepared foods at our fingertips, the temptations never really go away.

Mindfulness is a strong ally when it comes to changing our eating and living habits. It is easy for days to go by in a blur, as we get through what we need to do on autopilot and look forward to that moment at the end of a busy day when we can sit down for a couple of minutes. We often forget to have breakfast, grab lunch without thinking, and focus more on what we're going to do next rather than what we're doing right now. Often, we spend our time looking forward to those few days of relaxation and vacation each year, counting down the weeks to when we can finally put our feet up, only to then put pressure on ourselves to have the perfect vacation!

When you begin to cultivate mindfulness, you bring a little more calm and relaxation into everyday life, while at the same time being more observant about how you feel at any moment, noticing what and how you are eating and giving yourself a bit of space before making choices. At the end of a hard day's work, your body will all too easily rely on old habits for finding comfort, whether your habit happens to be ordering a pizza or having a glass of wine. All mindfulness does is allow you to observe those habits and the feelings or triggers attached to them so that you can then ask yourself what it is that you really want in order to feel good, to sleep well and wake up energized.

Mindfulness also encourages us to slow down while we are eating and instead of grabbing something on the run and hardly noticing what we are eating as we gulp it down, we turn off external distractions (yes, smartphones) and concentrate on our meal, enjoying each mouthful. When you respect food in this way, even if just for the few minutes it takes to have a meal, you respect your body and the relationship between the two.

Brian Wansink from Cornell University has conducted various studies on the relationship between our minds and our eating habits. In one, he was interested to find out what triggered people to stop eating, so he created a special soup bowl that could be continuously refilled via an invisible tube. His research team set up a table laid out half with bottomless bowls and half with normal bowls and let the participants sit down to eat and chat together for 20 minutes. They were then asked to give their opinions about the soup to the researchers. In just 20 minutes, those participants with a bottomless bowl had consumed an average of 75 percent more soup than those with regular bowls. This suggested that a major trigger that tells us to stop eating is when we have finished our food, rather than an awareness of how much we have eaten. So if we can improve our awareness and also keep an eye on the size of our portions, we have a good chance of improving our eating habits while enjoying what we are eating.

Conscious cleansing

You will notice quite a bit of variety in our soup cleanse recipes. This is partly because Nicole is a chef and loves the challenge of creating recipes that are delicious, healthy, and don't leave you feeling hungry, but also because variety keeps you mindful about what you are eating. You could easily eat the same two soups every day for a week and lose weight. The problem is that you won't have changed any long-term habits and you won't have had to think about what you're eating throughout the cleanse. With a variety of ingredients and choices, you're taking your diet and way of living into your own hands. As a result, you'll notice more easily how your body feels after eating certain foods, and what your body wants in order to feel really good.

Before you eat, take a few moments to use your senses to appreciate your meal. Breathe in the aromas of the food, take in its appearance with your eyes. As you cook, enjoy the rhythm of chopping and stirring, bringing ingredients and flavors together.

Writing things down always helps to make them stick in our minds and our habits. It may be as simple as keeping a food and exercise diary of everything you have eaten and how many steps you have taken during the day; this kind of awareness feeds our motivation. A vision board is also a great way to visualize a healthier lifestyle, with gorgeous photos of ingredients and recipes and places you'd like to go. This kind of gentle monitoring and checking in has been shown to help with changing habits for the long term.

Don't leave healthy habits entirely to the mercy of your willpower, as it's a finite resource that is easily used up, particularly by the usual stressful events that we need to tackle on a daily basis. Being prepared is one of the best ways to help your willpower; i.e., the fewer temptations you have in your cupboards at home and the more delicious healthy foods you have on hand, the better. Don't put off lunch, and never eat at your computer; the more you savor your food, the more nutrition you will absorb. A smile is half the meal.

Principles of the Soup Cleanse

Neither of us are dieticians or nutritionists, so we teamed up with Victoria Wells, who is a food-loving nutritionist. Nicole has a chef's instinct for balance in meals, while Kate has worked with experts across a wide range of disciplines always with a fascination for the relationship between how we feel and what we eat.

Different experts have different ideas about what exactly a cleanse might be, but for us it's a chance to give ourselves and our bodies the opportunity to rest, restore, and renew. A cleanse means taking some time to help our often-stressed digestive systems and our bodies regain their balance.

We instinctively lean toward the individualized approaches of traditional medicines such as Chinese and Ayurveda. In the more modern context, we understand the potential benefits of visiting a nutritionist or a health spa to help pinpoint strengths and weaknesses when it comes to diet and digestion. We also believe there is much we can do ourselves, in making choices that can improve how we feel, what we eat, and our overall relationship with food. For example, Kate has always had a relaxed relationship with food, but when she is stressed her healthy habits go haywire and she feels the same emotions about food as about whatever is stressing her! She has discovered that to regain her healthy relationship with her body and rebuild her digestive "fire," she also needs to give herself a break and chill out.

Whatever science tells us, our own experiences are equally great teachers. For example, some studies claim that drinking coffee is good for you, while others insist that you avoid it. The only person who really knows how coffee affects them, individually, is you. And it might change depending on how you are feeling, how busy you are, or what kind of shape your digestion is in. When you're working all hours, feeling low on energy, and reaching for cup after cup to keep yourself going, that's your body's way of telling you a no-caffeine cleanse is a good idea. (It really is surprising how quickly we lose the perceived need for coffee once it's out of our system.)

It's the same for things like wheat and gluten. Only people with celiac disease have a true gluten allergy and cannot tolerate it in any amount. For the rest of us, we need to decide for ourselves, or with the help of a nutritionist, if we feel better after cutting out gluten. Opting for breads made with rye, spelt, or a mix of grains grown on small farms and locally milled may not affect you in the same way.

A quick guide to the digestive system

It is through digestion that our body breaks down food into nutrients and absorbs what it needs to survive and thrive. A combination of the organs of the digestive system along with hormones, nerves, bacteria, and blood perform the complex task of digesting what we eat and drink. It is amazing what the digestive system can manage to cope with, but when we push things too far, we soon begin to suffer the consequences and feel less than 100 percent, both physically and mentally.

The digestive system is made up of the digestive or gastrointestinal (GI) tract and the liver, pancreas, and gallbladder. The GI tract begins with the mouth, then the esophagus, stomach, small intestine, and large intestine to the anus.

Digestion begins in the mouth, as we chew our food and release saliva, which moistens the food and contains an enzyme that begins to break down the starches in the food. Lingual lipase, a digestive enzyme, also starts the breakdown of fats in the mouth, although most food breakdown occurs in the small intestine. Even the speed at which we eat and chew is thought to have an effect on our digestion. If we can slow down while eating and take time to chew our food, we can make an instant, easy change for the benefit of the digestive system.

Once swallowed, the food passes through the esophagus to the stomach, where it is combined with gastric acid that contains an enzyme that breaks down the protein. The broken-down food is then slowly released from the stomach into the small intestine, where it is mixed with compounds from the pancreas that break down carbohydrates, fats, and proteins, and with bile from the liver that dissolves fats. Bacteria in the small intestine also produce enzymes to help digest carbohydrates. It is thought that these bacteria in particular, our gut flora, are affected by modern diet and lifestyles. You can have a positive effect on your gut health by eating fewer processed foods and opting for a variety of natural foods.

Digested nutrients are absorbed through the walls of the intestine into the bloodstream, which then carries those nutrients throughout the body. The waste products are pushed into the large intestine, where any water and remaining nutrients are absorbed. What's left is turned into stool to be stored in the rectum and then eliminated from the body in a bowel movement.

The body produces hormones that regulate appetite, signaling when we are hungry or full. We also have nerves that release chemicals that aid digestion.

Kidneys

While the kidneys are part of the urinary, rather than digestive, system, they are worth mentioning. The kidneys are responsible for removing waste and extra water from the blood once your body has taken the nutrients it needs from the food you eat. Generally, a diet rich in antioxidants is beneficial to kidney health. These include cruciferous vegetables (such as cabbage and cauliflower), the allium family (including garlic, onions, and leeks), as well as berries, apples, oily fish, and olive oil.

Signs of weakened digestion

When our digestive systems are under too much pressure, there are a number of signs that indicate that things aren't in optimal working order. These include:

- Bloating
- Flatulence
- Constipation
- Heartburn and indigestion
- Loose stools
- Fatigue
- Headaches

When any symptom persists for longer than two weeks, it is advisable to seek medical help. We give an outline of some of the common digestive system problems that many people experience at one time or another. There are entire books devoted to conditions like IBS and candida, so we only touch the surface here.

Bloating

Many women regularly experience the discomfort of bloating, particularly as the day goes on. It can be caused by overeating or eating too quickly, flatulence, constipation, candida overgrowth, water retention, or food intolerance. As with many digestive issues, it's a case of narrowing down the potential causes. If you read "eating too quickly" and think, "Oh, that's me," then focus on eating more slowly and chewing your food thoroughly for a while to see if it makes a difference. Likewise, if you don't like drinking water and probably only have a glass a day, substitute herbal teas or make naturally flavored waters (page 84) to increase your water intake and see if that helps. Dandelion tea, a natural diuretic that can work wonders with water retention, contains many nutrients and beneficial compounds, so it's great for a cleanse or enjoy a cup every now and then.

Too many carbonated drinks can cause bloating; steer clear of them while on a cleanse. Also, it is thought that raw food can trigger bloating for some people, which is why our recipes, like soups, are cooked to make foods more digestible.

Flatulence

Although adding more soluble fiber from fruits and vegetables is a good thing, one disadvantage is that doing so may cause increased intestinal gas. While some gas is natural, it does become problematic when it becomes excessive or has a bad smell. A probiotic or prescribed digestive enzymes can help. Drink a cup of chamomile tea after you eat; it may help to relieve gas.

Excessive gas may also be due to a mild but irritating food intolerance. If your digestive system is weakened, you can be intolerant to "healthy" foods such as beans, broccoli, cauliflower, Brussels sprouts, leeks, garlic, and onions. If you suspect this is the case, keep a food diary to help pinpoint the potential culprits and then try an elimination diet, where you avoid all the possible irritating foods. Then slowly introduce each food every three or four days, noting how they make you feel. Generally, if you begin to ease up on your digestive system by not overloading it, it will strengthen and might become tolerant once again to foods that previously triggered bloating and gas.

Constipation

What constitutes "regular" bowel movements is unique to each individual and can range from three times a day to three times a week. Anything less, though, is considered constipation and can start to feel extremely uncomfortable. There is plenty of fiber included in the cleanses, which, alongside drinking plenty of water and herbal teas throughout the day, should ensure good bowel movements. Soups are thought to be helpful, too, as is the avoidance of processed foods, and even giving yourself the time to go to the bathroom in a relaxed way rather than always in a rush.

Loose Stools

If you suffer from long-term bowel irregularities, visit your doctor or health care provider to rule out any infections or more serious conditions. Loose stools may be triggered by stress, anxiety, or specific foods. You can try eliminating these and then reintroducing them into your diet one at a time to see if one in particular is the specific cause. Common triggers are caffeine, dairy, high-saturated-fat foods such as red meat, and citrus fruit.

Kate has also found that taking a course of probiotics and a little apple cider vinegar at mealtimes helps improve her digestion. A nutritionist can give advice tailored to your personal situation.

Heartburn and Indigestion

Heartburn occurs when stomach acid is regurgitated and goes up into the esophagus, causing a burning sensation and chest tightness. Certain foods can make this worse, including fatty foods, alcohol, juices, chocolate, and, for some people, onions, garlic, and certain spices. Eating too much too fast can cause acid reflux, as can being overweight, so eating healthfully and mindfully is a good idea for preventing heartburn. Probiotics are thought to help, as are mint and chamomile teas.

Food Allergies and Intolerances

As a chef, Nicole has noticed over her career an increasing number of customers with food allergies and intolerances. She understands the importance of being notified about a customer's allergy to nuts or shellfish, or when a customer with celiac disease asks about gluten in a dish. Are more people becoming sensitive to dairy or gluten, or are we just more readily saying so now? Is being picky about specific ingredients a fad, or is it the way in which foods are processed that's made us intolerant?

You can always find evidence somewhere that will back up supposed allergies or intolerances. As food lovers, we opt for eating as much variety as possible, eating as little processed food as possible, and then trying to be aware of how foods make us feel as individuals. Kate finds peppers and cucumber skin "unsettling," while too much cow's milk tends to trigger indigestion for Nicole. We're very lucky, we know, because it's not hard to avoid peppers, cucumber skin, and milk, but perhaps there is something to be said for an attitude toward food that means we are excited to try everything. We also realize that there are times when we instinctively feel the need to simplify our diet and have a bowl of rice and vegetables. It's when we don't listen to our bodies that we end up with a food hangover.

Irritable Bowel Syndrome (IBS)

Although increasing numbers of people are reporting symptoms that are associated with IBS, it remains a difficult condition to diagnose, because there is no specific test. To reach a diagnosis of IBS is often quite a long journey of excluding other possible conditions, including Crohn's disease. IBS is termed a syndrome because it is a collection of symptoms, all or some of which may be experienced to varying degrees.

Symptoms of IBS include:

- Diarrhea
- Constipation
- Alternating diarrhea and constipation
- Abdominal cramps
- Bloating
- Flatulence
- Nausea
- Indigestion
- Mucous in stools
- Fatigue
- Headaches
- Backaches
- Sleep disruption
- Menstrual cramps
- Painful sex for women
- Mood swings
- Anxiety
- Depression

Often anxiety can trigger the physical symptoms of IBS, while the onset of a physical symptom such as diarrhea can in turn heighten anxiety, creating a negative cycle that is difficult to escape. Sufferers often feel both emotionally and physically exhausted, fearful of eating out in restaurants, and constantly on alert for flare-ups.

Obviously these symptoms are quite wide ranging, which makes it difficult to diagnose when someone is suffering from IBS and what is causing it so that positive steps can be taken. Note if your bowel habits change significantly for a period of time.

Although the exact causes of IBS haven't been established, there is still much that you can do (especially with the help of a nutritionist) to investigate possible causes and to begin to calm the symptoms through healthy eating habits—giving the gut a break from irritants, dealing with stress, and building a strong digestive system. It is thought that some cases of IBS are triggered by a previous case of food poisoning or gastrointestinal infection. Some people are thought to have more sensitive nerves in the bowel, so they need to look at whether particular foods trigger spasms and pain. For others, it might be related to antibiotics disrupting the healthy gut flora. Hormones can have an impact on symptoms, as can yeast overgrowth (*Candida albicans*).

The cleanses in this book are not designed to help with IBS specifically, but for simplifying your diet for a few days. Taking time out to rest and relax can be helpful both for calming the gut and beginning to pinpoint if any specific foods are causing sensitivity.

We have a friend whose digestive system broke down completely due to an infection and landed her in the hospital for months. Almost everything she tried to eat triggered IBS symptoms and pain. But over time, she decided that rather than live this way for the rest of her life, she would gradually build up her digestive system to be able to increase the variety of foods in her diet. She did such a good job that she now eats everything again in moderation. This isn't possible for everyone, of course, but it does show that sometimes there is a great deal we can do to help ourselves.

Which Cleanse Is Right for You?

A cleanse doesn't "detox" your body. Rather, the aim is to lighten the usual workload on your body's digestive system for a short period of time. If you provide your body with foods that are easier to digest and give yourself a break from the usual stresses and strains of daily life, you allow your body to rest, recuperate, and build up some of its energy reserves again.

For *The Ultimate Soup Cleanse*, we have created four cleanses, each with specific goals in mind.

1. RESOLVE

This 2-day cleanse is designed to resolve the problem of excess water retention and give your body a break from any foods that may be inflammatory. It is perfect for a quiet weekend when you want to balance out recent overindulgences. It's also a great way to kick-start a healthy weight-loss lifestyle change (particularly if you include the Rebalance cleanse), and an excellent reset for when you begin to feel yourself falling back into unhealthy habits. This cleanse is the perfect reminder for your body and mind of how great it feels to eat delicious, healthy food and take time to care for yourself.

GOALS

2 to 3 pounds weight loss (including excess water)
Banish excess bloat
Reset healthy habits
Take time out

2. REBALANCE

A 7-day weight-loss cleanse that begins with the Resolve kick-start weekend and continues in a gentler way through the week, with plenty of good fats and healthy protein to help retrain your appetite thermostat while eating a little less. It is possible to lose up to 7 pounds this week—4 pounds of which are likely to be excess water.

GOALS

5 to 7 pounds weight loss (including excess water)
Keep moving throughout the day
Try something new every day
Love food, love your body

A Healthy Weight for You

BMI

There is no 100 percent foolproof way to know what your healthy weight should be, but the Body Mass Index chart provides a healthy range.

Weight lb	100	105	110	115	120	125	130	135	140	145	150	155	160	165	170	175	180	185	190	195	200	205	210	215
Height	Underweight				Healthy					Overweight					Obese					Extremely obese				
5'0"	19	20	21	22	23	24	25	26	27	28	29	30	31	32	33	34	35	36	37	38	39	40	41	42
5'1"	18	19	20	21	22	23	24	25	26	27	28	29	30	31	32	33	34	35	36	36	37	38	39	40
5'2"	18	19	20	21	22	22	23	24	25	26	27	28	29	30	31	32	33	33	34	35	36	37	38	39
5'3"	17	18	19	20	21	22	23	24	24	25	26	27	28	29	30	31	32	33	34	35	36	36	37	38
5'4"	17	18	18	19	20	21	22	23	24	24	25	26	27	28	29	30	31	31	32	33	34	35	36	37
5'5"	16	17	18	19	20	20	21	22	23	24	25	25	26	27	28	29	30	30	31	32	33	34	35	35
5'6"	16	17	17	18	19	20	20	21	22	23	24	25	25	26	27	28	29	29	30	31	32	33	34	34
5'7"	15	16	17	17	18	19	20	20	21	22	23	24	25	25	26	27	28	29	29	30	31	32	33	34
5'8"	15	16	16	17	18	19	19	20	21	22	22	23	24	25	25	26	27	28	28	29	30	31	32	32
5'9"	14	15	16	17	17	18	19	20	20	21	22	22	23	24	25	25	26	27	28	28	29	30	31	31
5'10"	14	15	15	16	17	18	18	19	20	20	21	22	23	23	24	25	25	26	27	28	28	29	30	30
5"11"	14	14	15	16	16	17	18	18	19	20	21	21	22	23	23	24	25	25	26	27	28	28	29	30
6'0"	13	14	14	15	16	17	17	18	19	19	20	21	21	22	23	23	24	25	25	26	27	27	28	29
6'1"	13	13	14	15	15	16	17	17	18	19	19	20	21	21	22	23	23	24	25	25	26	27	27	28
6'2"	12	13	14	14	15	16	16	17	18	18	19	19	20	21	21	22	23	23	24	25	25	26	27	27
6'3"	12	13	13	14	15	15	16	16	17	18	18	19	20	20	21	21	22	23	23	24	25	25	26	26
6'4"	12	12	13	14	14	15	15	16	17	17	18	18	19	20	20	21	22	22	23	23	24	25	25	26

Underweight: below 18.5
Healthy range: 18.5–24.9
Overweight: 25–29.9
Obese: over 30

Waist to Hip Ratio

To calculate your waist-to-hip ratio, divide your waist measurement by your hip measurement. For women, ideally this number should be less than 0.8 and for men less than 0.95. The reason to check this is that it's an indication of whether you are carrying too much weight around your middle, which is thought to be more dangerous to your health than if you carry a bit of extra weight around your hips and butt area.

3. RESTORE

This is a 7-day cleanse focused on restoring and strengthening digestion. Since the brain and gut are connected, this is also a great way to improve mental concentration and focus. This cleanse lays healthy foundations for the long term by including restorative foods, such as bone broths and fermented foods, and restorative exercise that stokes your digestive fires from within.

GOALS

Relight digestive fire
Improve gut flora
Promote long-term healthy weight management
Regain clarity and mental focus

4. RENEW

A 5-day, nutrient-rich, energizing cleanse that is a great tune-up when you feel like you'd rather stay in bed and pull the covers over your head than go out for a run or a bike ride. Go for Renew when you'd like to get your joie de vivre back. It's always difficult to describe just what "vitality" is, but somehow we just know when we feel we have it and, conversely, when we're not quite firing on all cylinders.

GOALS

Replenish energy reserves
Wake up with vitality
Grab life with both hands

Frequently asked questions

Will I get headaches while on a cleanse?
You may get the odd headache when cutting out caffeine and sugar. It's surprising, however, how quickly our bodies get used to not having these stimulants. Challenge your willpower for the first two days, and it will become progressively easier to give up caffeine and sugar after that if you choose a longer cleanse.

Is it possible to shrink my stomach?
No, your stomach remains the same size no matter what you eat. You can, however, retrain your appetite so you feel satisfied after eating smaller portions. During the holiday seasons, it's easy to get used to eating more. It really helps if you eat slowly and mindfully, without distractions.

Should I avoid vegetables in the nightshade family?
Some nutrition experts believe the family of "nightshade" foods should be avoided. These include tomatoes, eggplant, potatoes, tomatillos, and peppers (bell peppers, chile peppers, and spices derived from these, such as cayenne and paprika). There is no research to suggest that they are a problem for most people, but if you feel you are sensitive to them, talk to a nutritionist to find out more.

How much weight can I expect to lose?
It depends how much retained water you lose. Some people will lose up to 7 pounds in the first week, of which 4 pounds is likely to be water and 2 to 3 pounds fat.

What if I become constipated?
There is plenty of fiber included in the cleanse recipes, so you should be fine, but sometimes our digestive systems aren't keen on change. Try to stay relaxed about it—Kate's best home remedy to get things moving is a teaspoon of molasses.

Should I take nutritional supplements?
It's best to talk to a medical practitioner or a nutritionist about whether you would benefit from any specific supplements. We do take a quality probiotic supplement to help build up the beneficial bacteria when our digestion feels weakened.

What about "superfoods"?
"Superfoods" are a marketing gimmick. All fruits and vegetables are great for you. You're as likely to absorb as many nutrients from broccoli and kale as you are from spirulina. If you happen to like any particular so-called superfoods, then go for them.

Should I see a nutritionist?
Seeing a registered nutritionist or dietitian can be helpful if you suspect you may be suffering from a digestive condition or you need some tailored help with your diet. Using the Internet to look up various symptoms is more likely to raise questions than provide answers. Having a professional consider your whole health picture can be very helpful.

What if I think I'm intolerant to foods on the cleanse?
We are all unique when it comes to our reactions to food, so feel free to tweak the cleanses if there are ingredients that don't agree with you. We have deliberately included a wide variety of foods and haven't been overly restrictive. For example, some people may find it difficult to digest legumes. Use the additional recipes at the back of the book to inspire your taste buds and see what you really like.

Preparations

We often tell ourselves "tomorrow I'm going to change my behavior and eat only healthy foods." But when tomorrow comes and the fridge is empty or, even worse, there's a bar of chocolate lurking in the cupboard, our healthy intentions quickly fly out the window.

The more prepared we are, the easier we find it to adopt and stick with healthy habits. Get the spice cabinet fully stocked, fill the fridge with jars of vegetable and chicken stock, clear kitchen work surfaces, and pin your menus for the week somewhere you can easily see them.

Kitchen cleanse

Nicole definitely believes in the "life-changing magic of tidying up" approach that Marie Kondo writes about in her bestselling book of the same name. When you think about it, it's much easier to work on a clean desk, clear of clutter, with one task at hand in front of you. Even our minds become full of clutter that we no longer need—old hurts and hang-ups, tensions and worries. Nicole loves to have clear surfaces and organized cupboards before she begins to create. When preparing for a cleanse, it really helps to clean out your cupboards and fridge so you can look forward to stocking up and cooking some nourishing recipes over the next few days.

Soup Equipment

The good news about making soup is that it's much easier to clean up afterward than it is when you are juicing—all that pulp that just seems to stick to the equipment! Plus, that's the fiber—the good stuff is being thrown away. When making soups, your best friend is a blender, followed by an assortment of glass and plastic containers. You can make batches of soup over the weekend for the week ahead, so all you need to do is heat them up and add a few nuts and seeds when you're ready to eat. Easy.

Blenders

We have tested all kinds of blenders over the years, and we find that the simple ones seem to work the best for us. A handheld immersion blender makes cleanup easy. If using a standing blender, allow the soup to cool for a bit before blending so the steam doesn't build up, causing the lid to pop off. Also, work in batches, filling the blender just halfway, so nothing overflows when the machine is turned on.

Insulated Food Containers

We love wide-brimmed insulated Thermos jars, like those from Black + Blum, for keeping hot soups hot and cold soups cold while on the go. If you are able to heat up your soup at work during the day, there are some great plastic containers and glass jars available.

Storage

Nicole tends to put everything into plastic containers or glass jars. We each have a cupboard neatly stacked with just about every size container you could think of. Nicole's best tip is to try to find the size that leaves the least room for air at the top—that way your soup (or whatever else you are storing) will last for a day or two longer.

Pantry essentials

While this may look like a long list, all these ingredients keep well and form the basis of a cupboard of healthy foods and condiments that you can fall back on any day of the week.

Extra-virgin olive oil
Coconut oil
Peanut oil
Sesame seeds black and white
Chia seeds
Flaxseed meal
Hemp seeds
Pumpkin seeds
Almonds
Almond butter
Tamari (wheat-free soy sauce)
Turmeric, ground or fresh
Cumin seeds
Fennel seeds
Mustard seeds·
Caraway seeds
Cloves, ground
Cinnamon, ground
Cayenne
Nori (seaweed) flakes
Kombu (seaweed) sheets
Miso paste, brown and white

Shiitake mushrooms, dried and
    fresh
Apple cider vinegar
Olives
Capers
Preserved lemons
Quinoa, white, red, or black
Oatmeal
Rice, brown and wild
Buckwheat groats
Brown rice noodles
Buckwheat noodles
Chickpeas, dried
Mung beans
Adzuki beans
Split peas
Red lentils
Le Puy lentils
Fennel tea
Dandelion tea
Green sencha tea
Raw honey

Friends of the soup cleanse

Which key foods will bring you the most nutrients? Well, it turns out that the best diet you can give your body is a varied one that includes whole foods such as vegetables, fruit, lean protein, whole grains, herbs and spices, legumes (beans and lentils), nuts and seeds, probiotics (fermented foods such as kimchi and sauerkraut), and live cultures (such as yogurt and kefir). A combination of these foods provides a diet rich in antioxidants, fiber, and pre- and probiotics that create the best environment for the good bacteria in our guts to flourish. Creating the optimum environment means that we absorb nutrients from our food, release energy at a steady pace, and eliminate waste effectively.

Antioxidants

Antioxidants are chemicals that interact with and neutralize free radicals, or act as scavengers, helping to prevent cell damage. They are widely accepted by both conventional and alternative health practitioners to be beneficial for our health.

There is a whole range of good chemicals within the antioxidant family that are contained in a variety of foods:

- Vitamin C in berries and greens
- Vitamin E in vegetable oils, nuts, and avocado
- Beta-carotene in squash and carrots
- Copper in beans and lentils
- Manganese in nuts
- Lycopene in tomatoes
- Polyphenols in herbs
- Selenium in fish, meat, and whole grains
- Allium sulfur compounds in garlic, onions, and leeks
- Anthocyanins in eggplant

- Catechins in red wine and tea
- Flavonoids in green tea, citrus fruit, and apples
- Indoles in cruciferous vegetables such as cabbage, cauliflower, and broccoli
- Lutein in leafy greens and corn
- Zinc in seafood, lean meat, and nuts

Fiber for Gut Health

Fiber is essential for digestive health, which is why we've included plenty of fiber-rich ingredients in our recipes. Dietary fiber is an umbrella term used to group together the components of food that can't be digested and are therefore eliminated as waste in our bowel movements.

The two main forms of fiber are soluble—sources include oats, beans, and fruits—and insoluble, and are found in whole wheat, nuts, seeds, and some vegetables. The soluble fiber is broken down in the colon while the insoluble fiber remains mainly solid, although it is still fermented to a degree by bacteria in the digestive system. In his book *The Diet Myth*, Tim Spector assesses all the studies related to fiber (and many other food components) to try to understand why fiber does indeed seem like a good thing to include in our diet when it doesn't appear to do much except create waste. He discovered that the answer may lie in microbes, and in particular, prebiotics. Prebiotics act as fertilizers for our body's own microbes and allow good bacteria to thrive. All prebiotics are indigestible fiber or carbohydrates, including:

- Asparagus
- Endive
- Broccoli
- Dandelion greens
- Garlic
- Jerusalem artichokes
- Leeks
- Onions

Other fiber-rich foods include:

- Avocado
- Barley
- Chia seeds
- Flaxseed meal
- Oats

- Split peas
- Lentils
- Peas

Lentils and beans

Some people find lentils and beans difficult to digest and may experience cramps, bloating, and/or excess gas after eating them. Here are some tips for making them more digestible.

Soaking—instead of soaking them in water for the usual "overnight," soak them for 48 hours and change the water three times a day.

Sprouting (page 62)—sprouted beans are easier to digest.

Slow-cooking—cook your lentils and beans for as long as possible on the lowest heat.

Kombu—put a strip of kombu seaweed in while they are soaking and a fresh strip while cooking. Remove the kombu before serving.

Probiotics

The health of the microbes, or "gut flora" or "good bacteria," in your digestive system appears to have a strong correlation both with digestive health and overall health and well-being. The good news is that both tradition and science offer some easy and delicious ways to improve gut flora.

Fermentation, an ancient method of preserving food, has seen a resurgence, both in the culinary world and that of health promoters—it's nice when that happens. Foods like sauerkraut and kefir act in the same ways as probiotic supplements by improving your digestive health. The more friendly bacteria we can create in the world, the better.

Probiotic foods include:

- Kefir
- Kimchi
- Kombucha
- Live yogurt (the container should say "live and active cultures")
- Miso
- Sauerkraut

Fasting and snacking

It is thought that giving your body's microbes a balance of work and rest by fasting—not eating for periods of time—is a good idea. We naturally fast when sleeping, between our evening meal and breakfast. There is, however, a growing school of thought that suggests that when we eat a healthy diet, we don't need to worry so much about snacking to prevent blood sugar drops, cravings, and biting other people's heads off.

The secret is to get to know your own circadian rhythm, which begs the question, are you a morning or an evening person? If you do all your best work in the morning and find you would rather rest quietly in the evening, you don't need so much energy—in other words, food—later in the day. You may find that out of habit, boredom, or the need for a reward you eat every time you have a break, when really a cup of herbal tea would be fine until lunch or dinner. If you are an evening person—for example, you find that you are alert and happy to work when most people have gone home for the day—you won't necessarily need to eat a huge breakfast.

This is something you can practice while on the cleanse, because during it you will become more mindful of how you feel and what your body needs.

Anti-inflammatory foods

Inflammation is specifically associated with conditions such as arthritis, chronic pain, and gastrointestinal disorders, including Crohn's disease and ulcerative colitis. A healthy diet that includes anti-inflammatory foods is of potential benefit to such conditions. Prevention of symptoms is best, since there are no cures for these inflammatory diseases and disorders. By taking steps to maintain a healthy diet and lifestyle, we can help ourselves take care of our own health. It is impossible to predict what health issues we may meet in our lifetimes, but being proactive without being obsessive seems like a good idea.

- Turmeric, a plant root, is one of the most powerful natural anti-inflammatory ingredients known at present. Ground turmeric is sold in the spice section at your grocery store, while fresh turmeric is available in the specialty and ethnic market.
- Ginger root is also an anti-inflammatory and antioxidant.
- Seaweed is an underwater gem. For centuries, people who live along coastal waters have dried edible seaweed for its minerals and rich nutritional content. Seaweeds, or sea vegetables, contain minerals and energy-boosting B vitamins, which are good for the brain and skin and also strengthen the immune system. Nori is one of the few vegetables that contains long-chain omega-3 fatty acids, which are particularly effective against inflammation.
- Cold-water oily fish such as salmon, tuna, mackerel, sardines, and anchovies contain anti-inflammatory omega-3 fatty acids.
- Antioxidant-rich fruit and vegetables, particularly the carotenoids in carrots, sweet potatoes, and squash, and the allium family of garlic, onion, and leek.
- Monounsaturated fats found in extra-virgin olive oil, nuts, and avocado.

Natural diuretics

There are a number of herbs and foods that are thought to help reduce water retention and/or bloating, so we have included these in some of *The Ultimate Soup Cleanse* recipes:

Adzuki beans	Horseradish
Alfalfa	Kohlrabi
Asparagus	Leek
Barley	Lemon
Basil	Mung beans
Buckwheat	Pea
Caraway seeds	Radish
Celery	Seaweed
Corn	Squash
Fennel	Watercress

Why we prefer organic, local, and seasonal food

It isn't just choosing the food itself that matters when we make decisions about what we eat, it's also how it was grown, raised, or produced and how far it had to travel to reach our tables. Many people believe that organic food is just more expensive and that there are no tangible benefits to buying it. We see organic food not only as a way to consume fewer toxins, but also to support a method of farming and producing that is more sustainable for the land and for the most part is more ethical in its treatment of animals.

In the United States, and increasingly in Europe and elsewhere, it is possible to know if the beef you are buying was grass-fed rather than being reared in barns and fed only corn enhanced with antibiotics and hormones. As far as the argument about organic foods being more expensive goes, we have discovered that farm shops and farmers' markets often sell organic vegetables for less than the price of conventionally grown produce in supermarkets. Organic meat is expensive, though, as it should be, so we try to make it go a long way.

Foods to avoid

These are divided into two groups. The first are foods that are probably best avoided whenever possible, except for celebrations and vacations—try for 80 percent of the time. These include processed foods and also refined sugar. Then there are the foods that really depend on your own constitution, and the context and amounts in which they are eaten. For example, we are not against wheat or dairy, but we do understand that they are the kinds of foods that we can easily overeat and therefore become a little sensitive to. Some people are, of course, lactose intolerant and unable to digest dairy foods, but for the majority of us it is a case of finding the balance that feels right individually. We often find that once we give our digestion a little rest and recovery time, we are able to enjoy a wider range of foods once again without the digestive problems that we were previously experiencing.

Processed Foods

It's difficult to lump all processed foods into one "bad" category, because some foods—like quinoa and buckwheat groats (kasha)—are processed in some form before they reach the shelf.

The kinds of processed foods we are talking about are cookies, sweetened cereals, chocolate bars, potato and tortilla chips, processed meats (including most sausages and bacon), processed cheese, packaged bread, and yogurts with fruit syrups or any additives other than milk. Many fast-food and takeout restaurants sell processed foods, and however healthy they claim to be, most of them aren't all that natural when you read the ingredient labels. And that's the key: check the ingredients of foods before you buy them, and if you're not sure about any of them, take a pass.

Sugar

Sugar has gotten such a bad rap in recent years that many people have become concerned about eating any sugar, including the sugar in fruit. It's not the naturally occurring sugar in fresh fruit that is the problem—it's the ways in which refined sugar has crept into the average diet, and that does include fruit juices made from concentrate or those with added sugar.

There is still a debate over whether sugar is now the predominant cause of obesity, but the proponents of this theory are beginning to line up, especially when you consider the rise in childhood obesity. In the United Kingdom, currently 10 percent of children are obese when they start primary school, and by the time they leave primary school the figure doubles to 20 percent. According to Rachel K. Johnson, lead author of a paper published in the American Heart Association (AHA) journal *Circulation,* too much sugar not only makes people fat but is also a key culprit in diabetes, high blood pressure, heart disease, and stroke.

Watch out for added sugar, also called sucrose, fructose, or high-fructose corn syrup, in:

- Low-fat foods
- Jams and jellies
- Salad dressings
- Marinades
- Baked goods
- Bread
- Cereals
- Yogurt
- Fruit juice
- Fruit-flavored waters
- Pizza
- Margarine
- Sauces in jars
- Breakfast bars
- Prepared meals

Artificial Sweeteners

There are many artificial sweeteners, designed to help people consume less sugar. While our personal preference is to eat natural foods, we also prefer to avoid artificial or natural but highly processed sweeteners. There is some evidence to suggest that choosing low-calorie options, in particular carbonated drinks, does nothing to help people lose weight. Some nutrition experts explain that when we consume artificial sweeteners, we are doing nothing to retrain our sweet tooth, and will therefore continue to crave sweet, high-calorie foods such as cakes and cookies. Artificial sweeteners may also alter the gut microbiome balance, so are best avoided.

Artificial sweeteners include:

- Acesulfame potassium
- Aspartame
- Mannitol
- Neotame
- Sucralose
- Saccharin
- Sorbitol
- Xylitol

Natural sweeteners include:

- Agave nectar
- Coconut or palm sugar
- Molasses
- Stevia leaf extract
- Raw honey
- Raw maple syrup

When you start looking into refined sugar and its natural alternatives, things can become confusing. Just a few years ago, agave nectar was hailed as the healthiest natural alternative to sugar, until it was discovered to contain extremely high levels of fructose, much more than honey, for example.

Our favorite natural sweeteners are raw honey and coconut or palm sugar, which has been processed less than refined white sugar. "Raw" honey doesn't go through the same processing and pasteurization methods as other honey and so retains more of its natural probiotics and enzymes. Honey contains a better balance of fructose *and* glucose than refined table sugar, so is more easily assimilated by the body. It is still best to eat it in small quantities, however, but a spoonful on your oatmeal is just fine.

Alcohol

Alcohol seems to us a bit like caffeine: when we're on vacation, it's part of eating out and having fun, but when we're working hard, it saps our energy levels or alertness. If you do enjoy a glass of wine or three, especially over the holidays, then cutting out alcohol while on the cleanses gives you an immediate energy boost, especially in the morning, and you will likely find that you sleep much more soundly. Of course, alcohol is hard work for the liver, and not drinking is the best tonic you can give it, which is why we avoid it during the cleanses.

Caffeine

Caffeine isn't necessarily bad for you, but during the cleanses we suggest replacing it with herbal teas. Green tea does have a little caffeine in it, but it doesn't affect the body in the same way as coffee does. Our aim with a cleanse is to bring ourselves back into balance and also improve our sleep patterns. Cutting down on caffeine is a helpful way to do that.

Dairy

There are many unprocessed cheeses, as well as live yogurts and kefirs, that contain lots of beneficial bacteria, which may be one of the reasons why the French diet is considered to be so healthy, despite at first glance looking as though it is full of all the wrong things: saturated fats in butter, milk, cheese, and red meat, plus all that wine, croissants, and bread. The thing is that most French people eat these foods in moderation and enjoy small amounts that are a natural part of their culture. We have replaced cow's milk and butter with other ingredients during the cleanses, again to give the digestive system a break from rich foods. We are not against these foods in general, and believe butter to be a food of the gods!

Trade-offs

Try to swap extra-virgin olive or nut oils (such as coconut, peanut, or sesame) for butter. As we've said, we are not anti-butter—our philosophy is to eat and enjoy a wide variety of natural foods—but during a cleanse we forgo butter since it is harder to digest than olive and nut oils. Olive oil, in particular, contains many health-giving properties. Olive oil is at the heart of the Mediterranean diet, considered to be one of the healthiest in the world. Many of the health-promoting benefits attributed to the Mediterranean diet are related to consuming olive oil, including helping to reduce the risk of heart disease and certain cancers.

Yogurt and kefir in place of cream: Like butter, cream is high in saturated fat and so quite difficult to digest. (We know that sinking, uncomfortable feeling after a restaurant meal cooked with cream.) We now prefer lighter, and also probiotic, options such as plain Greek yogurt and kefir. We have also discovered that you can blend tofu into a vegetable soup for creaminess (honestly), which also adds some protein.

Nut, rice, or soy milks in place of cow's milk: For the cleanse we have gone for dairy-free foods (except for plain Greek yogurt and kefir, because they contain beneficial bacteria). There are so many delicious and varied alternatives to dairy milk now, and our favorites are the nut milks: coconut, almond, and hazelnut. Go for unsweetened varieties with no emulsifiers.

Wheat . . . and Gluten

Like so many people, we generally try to eat fewer foods containing wheat, finding that when we consume too much bread, pizza, and pasta, we feel bloated and uncomfortable. That's why the cleanses are wheat-free. Instead, the cleanses include seeds like quinoa and buckwheat, which are also gluten-free, and grains including rice, oats, and barley. Rice and oats are naturally gluten-free, but oats are often processed alongside wheat, so you have to look for noncontaminated varieties labeled "gluten-free." Barley contains gluten, but is also a natural diuretic.

Gluten seems to be another food enemy of choice right now. About 1 percent of the population is thought to suffer from celiac disease, an autoimmune reaction to gluten that can only be alleviated by eliminating gluten entirely from the diet. In recent years, however, the rise of a newly named condition—"non-celiac gluten sensitivity"—has grabbed the headlines and fed the expansion of the "free-from" food industry.

The trouble is that the symptoms of any food intolerance are similar: bloating, cramps, flatulence, and irregular bowel movements. The only way to really know which foods are causing the symptoms is to exclude or eliminate these foods from your diet for a period of time and then carefully reintroduce them. This means you stop eating any of the potential trigger foods for twenty-eight days and then reintroduce them one at a time to discover which one(s) you are sensitive to. This takes a huge commitment, and it's easy to see why it might seem simpler to just cut out both wheat and gluten.

It might be that we are just greedy food lovers at heart, but we're not keen on cutting out any whole foods, so we focus on the way ingredients are used and processed to keep our diet as varied as possible. We ban supermarket bread from our cupboards, but we will buy a loaf of sourdough from local bakers who mill their own flour. We have no scientific basis for it, but we also find no digestive issues with baguettes from the *boulangerie* in France or a starter portion of fresh pasta while in Italy. The old adage "When in Rome . . ." works well for us, as food rules go.

Red Meat

To give the digestive system a break from its usual workload, we do not include red meat in its whole form during the cleanse, but bone broth is included in the Restore and Renew cleanses. Think of red meat as many cultures do: a rich food that is full of nutrients to be enjoyed in modest amounts. When you think of meat in this way, it makes sense to look for the best-quality meat available, which for us means meat raised not too far away, grass-fed, and organic.

Enhancing the cleanse

In this section we have included some ways in which you can enhance the effects of the cleanse. Eating natural foods will benefit your skin from within. You may find that your eyes become brighter, your skin more radiant, and your hair and nails healthier. You can also take this time to try out other healthy rituals such as body brushing, oil pulling, salt baths, and meditation.

Body Brushing

Body, or skin, brushing is something you can do every day to help stimulate circulation. Just as the liver and kidneys are organs of elimination, we excrete and eliminate waste products through our skin.

Skin brushing is also thought to support the lymphatic system, which, like the bloodstream, goes all through our bodies. Lymph works as a major filtering system for the body and helps fight infections as part of the immune system.

How to Body Brush
Do this on dry skin for a couple of minutes before you shower.

- Purchase a natural-bristle brush, ideally with a long handle so you can reach your back.
- Don't brush your face or anywhere that feels tender. Women shouldn't brush their breasts.
- Start gently.
- Always brush toward your heart.
- Start with the soles of your feet and up each leg.
- Brush from the hands along your arms to your shoulders.
- Brush upward on the buttocks and lower back.
- Use a gentle motion on the tummy toward the center of your torso.
- Brush from the back of the neck to the front and gently on the chest toward the heart (just to repeat—avoid the breasts).

(*Note:* If you have any medical condition, check with your doctor first before body brushing.)

Oil Pulling

This is an oral hygiene cleansing technique with origins in Ayurvedic medicine. It is said to draw out toxins, improving oral health and overall health, too. There are no scientific studies to support this theory, but anecdotally, people report whiter teeth, cured hangovers, and better breath.

43

How to Oil Pull:

- The practice involves gently swishing 1 teaspoon of cold-pressed oil, such as organic coconut oil, around the mouth for 20 minutes in the morning on an empty stomach. It doesn't have to be a vigorous action, just keep it gently moving around and make sure it reaches all the nooks and crannies of your mouth. The liquid does increase in volume as it mixes with your saliva, so try only a little to start with, and make sure you don't swallow any of it.
- After 20 minutes, spit out the liquid and rinse out your mouth with a teaspoon of salt dissolved in warm water.

Epsom Salt Baths

Epsom salt is named after a saline spring at Epsom, in Surrey, England, and is a naturally occurring mineral compound of magnesium and sulfate. Studies have shown that these minerals are readily absorbed through the skin and may help with the elimination of toxins. You can find Epsom salt in drug stores everywhere. Dissolve one to two cups in your bath water.

An Epsom salt bath a couple of times a week brings many benefits:

- Helps with inflammation
- Eases stress and relaxes the body
- Relieves aches and pains
- Improves the body's absorption of nutrients
- May help relieve constipation

Breathing Exercise

This exercise gives your mind and body a few minutes of rest. In this breathing meditation, use the breath so that the physical body may help calm the mind, and vice versa, in a cycle of focused relaxation.

Find a space that feels light and open to you to help your mind feel open. Sit either on the floor or on a cushion on the floor, or in a straight-backed chair with your feet comfortably resting on the ground about shoulder width apart. Rest your hands in your lap in a comfortable position.

Check your posture. You should be sitting:

- Cross-legged
- Back straight (imagine a stack of coins)
- Shoulders stretched slightly outward, like the wings of a bird
- Neck slightly bent
- Eyes open, focused slightly down in front of you
- Mouth slightly open, with the tip of your tongue touching your upper palate
- Hands in your lap, in a comfortable position

Now simply sit for a few moments and just be. Allow yourself to settle into your body and your position; let things become quiet. Begin to focus on your breath, gently breathing in and out. Don't hold your breath on the inhale; just let it go out again at a pace that feels comfortable to you. Bring your mind to the breath—you might want to imagine tensions going out of your body on the out breath, or just focus on the rhythm of your inhalation and exhalation.

Your thoughts will still continue to rise up—don't worry about your mind wandering during this exercise. Observe your thoughts as they appear, acknowledge them, then let them go, and bring your attention back to your breath. Focusing on the breath like this for even just a few breaths before eating will immediately bring a sense of calm and may help to slow things down so you can eat mindfully and enjoy every bite. It is a great daily practice for relieving tension and allowing the stresses of the day to wash away.

Meditation on the Body

In this meditation, you allow your mind to take care of your body and bathe it in your appreciation. It's easiest to do this meditation lying down, with your eyes closed and your arms resting in a relaxed position by your sides.

Breathe gently in and out, just as you did in the first breathing exercise. Breathe from your belly and begin to sense all the places where your body is touching the bed or the floor—really feel those points of contact and allow yourself to sink downward, feeling heavy and grounded.

Bring your focus back to the breath and the rise and fall of your stomach. Keep your attention there for a few moments before taking your mind on a journey around the body. You can start with your toes; imagine breathing positive energy or light in through the tips of your toes and through your feet. How are your feet feeling? Sense any tension and breathe with it; imagine your feet are completely relaxed.

Now come up through your ankles to your calves and then your knees. Observe any feelings of tension or pain and continue to bathe your legs in positive energy.

Bring your focus to all the different parts of your body, your hands, your chest, shoulders, back and neck, your face, your forehead, and the crown of your head. Send your appreciation through your breath to all the far corners of your body and send love to any places of pain or tension.

You may also want to focus on your different organs and the amazing tasks they perform, and your senses, too—being able to taste wonderful foods, see the world, and listen to a friend. These are a few minutes in which you can observe and connect with whatever it is you are thankful for in your body.

At the end of the meditation, bring your focus back to breathing in and out, back to your belly. Open your eyes slowly and stretch before calmly getting up. This is an easy and relaxing meditation to do while on any of the cleanses, or even every day.

Cleansing is the perfect way to give yourself permission to take care of yourself, to take a little time to nourish your body and mind. It's like a reminder to yourself that healthy eating and healthy living feel really good, that to wake up in the morning feeling refreshed is the perfect start to the day. It resets your sense of balance, and you feel lighter all around. So let's get to them!

The Cleanses

....

RESOLVE

2-day ultimate cleanse

Put aside a quiet weekend for this 2-day cleanse. Allow yourself to rest and relax during the day, and treat yourself to an essential oil bath (our favorite is rose) one evening and an Epsom salt bath on another.

The ingredients in this cleanse will help with excess water retention and are anti-inflammatory and gently nourishing. The soups are light, which is why this is just a 2-day cleanse. It is designed to give your body a break from its usual workload. Give yourself a break at the same time and think of this cleanse as your own personal retreat. Read a book, go for quiet walks, or, if you enjoy yoga, do some stretches between meals.

Tips for the RESOLVE cleanse:

- Allow 12 hours between dinner the first night and breakfast the following day to give your digestive system plenty of downtime.

- Combine calming activities, such as reading, meditation, or simply sitting in the sunshine, with some gentle exercise, such as walking and yoga.
- Drink cleansing teas, such as green, fennel, and dandelion, throughout the day.
- Body brush (see page 43) in the morning.
- Turn off your electronic devices for the weekend.

2-DAY RESOLVE MENU

(Note: Substituting the ingredient in parentheses will make the dish vegan.)

DAY 1
Lemon juice, mint, and hot water
Miso breakfast broth
Turmeric, ginger, and lemongrass broth
Leeks and fennel with red lentils (double batch)
Almond chia smoothie
Hot cucumber with salmon (or quinoa)

DAY 2
Lemon juice, mint, and hot water
Miso breakfast broth
Turmeric, ginger, and lemongrass broth
Balti-spiced cauliflower
Leeks and fennel with red lentils

....

REDUCE AND REBALANCE

7-day weight-loss cleanse

This cleanse is designed to follow the 2-day Resolve cleanse and continues for the remaining 5 days of the week with a menu that helps banish bloating or water retention and begins to burn fat. The results will be different for each individual but expect to lose 3 to 7 pounds during the 7 days. Meals throughout the week are light but sustaining, with plenty of lean protein, good fats, and spices.

Our aim when we need to lose those holiday pounds is to recharge our desire for delicious, healthy ingredients and reset our appetite. It's all too easy to fall into the habit of continual grazing, but it's not a bad thing to allow ourselves to feel hungry rather than instantly feed our seemingly bottomless appetite.

This is a week where it's important to bring together the mind and the body. Sustained weight loss takes a firm commitment at the beginning, attention to and awareness of what and how we are eating and living as we lose the weight, and finding the healthy things we enjoy and can fall back on for the long term. Kate lost 35 pounds 5 years ago and has maintained that weight loss by walking for exercise and never letting store-bought ready-to-eat meals back into her life. And whenever she feels the need to get back into healthier habits, she makes a big pot of kitchari.

Tips for the REDUCE AND REBALANCE cleanse:

- On waking, drink a cup of hot water with lemon juice. Drink your favorite herbal teas throughout the day to help reduce any lingering water retention and stave off hunger.
- Be as active as possible. Walk whenever possible and include at least 60 minutes of cardio exercise per week. Lifting kettlebells or weight, or doing Zumba, Spinning, or CrossFit are all great choices.

- Try not to snack every midmorning and afternoon, but if you really feel you may cave in to sweet cravings if you don't have a snack, eat a Nourish Bite (page 82).
- Keep a food and mood diary through the week (and ideally beyond) to become more aware of what you are eating and how foods affect your energy and mood.
- Find time to eat without the distractions of work or the television. Eat slowly and mindfully.

7-DAY REDUCE AND REBALANCE MENU

PREPARE AHEAD
Roast chicken
Chicken stock
Vegetable stock
Seaweed broth

DAY 1
Lemon juice, mint, and hot water
Miso breakfast broth
Turmeric, ginger, and lemongrass broth
Leeks and fennel with red lentils (double batch)
Almond chia smoothie
Hot cucumber with salmon (or quinoa)

DAY 2
Lemon juice, mint, and hot water
Miso breakfast broth
Turmeric, ginger, and lemongrass broth
Balti-spiced cauliflower
Leeks and fennel with red lentils

DAY 3
Lemon juice and hot water (with optional teaspoon of honey)
Overnight grains with yogurt and apple
Seaweed broth (or Miso)
Zucchini, lemon, and thyme (double batch)
Coconut chicken with kale (or Sprouted soup)

DAY 4
Lemon juice and hot water
Overnight grains with nuts and berries
Lime and mint water
Zucchini, lemon, and thyme
Sichuan chicken (or tofu)

DAY 5
Lemon juice and hot water
Miso breakfast grains
Coconut water
Lemon, chicken, and mint (or adzuki bean kitchari)
Turmeric, ginger, and lemongrass broth
Asparagus mimosa

DAY 6
Lemon juice and hot water
Overnight grains with nuts and berries
Avocado on rye
Butternut squash and horseradish (double batch)
Kitchari with sautéed spinach

DAY 7
Lemon juice and hot water (with optional teaspoon of honey)
Egg drop with nori
Butternut squash, lemon, and sage
Turmeric, ginger, and lemongrass broth
Kitchari with shrimp or Greek yogurt

RESTORE

7-day cleanse for restoring and strengthening digestion

Digestion is the key to your vitality and sense of well-being. Even if you're eating nutrient-dense foods, you may not be digesting them well, and if so, your body won't be able to absorb those nutrients. If you are experiencing a great deal of stress in your life, for example, all that stress will put pressure on your immune system and potentially cause inflammation. You might develop food sensitivities or suffer from symptoms such as headaches, body aches, and frequent tiredness.

In today's world, symptoms associated with a weakened digestive system are becoming more widely felt by increasing numbers of otherwise healthy people. Blended soups are particularly good for nourishing and strengthening a weakened digestive system, as the food is already warmed and has been partially broken down in the blender. This isn't to say that we don't also see the potential benefits of including raw food in the diet, but from personal experience, we know that when our digestive system is in need of a little help, eating more warm foods is a good idea, especially later in the day.

Tips for the RESTORE cleanse:

- Eat slowly and without distractions.
- Take a probiotic to help your gut flora flourish and absorb more nutrients from the foods you eat.
- Eat a healthy breakfast in the mornings and lighter meals in the evenings. Don't overeat.
- Eat fresh, seasonal, and ideally local produce.
- Add raw foods later in the week as your digestion feels strengthened.
- Do moderate exercise and practice deep breathing.
- Get a massage.

7-DAY RESTORE MENU

PREPARE AHEAD
Vegetable stock
Roast chicken
Chicken stock
Bone broth or Seaweed broth
Nourish bites
White kimchi
Overnight oats

DAY 1
Lemon juice and hot water
Bircher overnight oats
Miso
Celeriac and mustard with seeded quinoa (double batch)
Nourish bite
Sesame chicken or Avocado, corn, and kale

DAY 2
Lemon juice and hot water
Almond chia smoothie
Celeriac and mustard with seeded quinoa
Chicken congee or Avocado, corn, and kale

DAY 3
Lemon juice and hot water
Miso breakfast broth
Asparagus barley with an egg
Bone broth (Seaweed broth)
Magic soup with kefir (double batch)

DAY 4
Lemon juice and hot water
Egg drop with nori
Nourish bite (optional)
Sweet potato, onion, and pomegranate molasses (double batch)
Bone broth (or Seaweed broth)
Magic soup with spinach and spiced onion

DAY 5
Lemon juice and hot water
Overnight oats with nuts and berries
Almond butter and apple on rye, or Nourish bite
Sweet potato, onion, and pomegranate molasses
White kimchi with buckwheat noodles

DAY 6
Lemon juice and hot water
Miso breakfast grains
Sprouted soup (double batch)
Nourish bite
Curried parsnip and apple (double batch)

DAY 7
Lemon juice and hot water
Egg drop with nori
Sprouted soup
Bone broth (or Seaweed broth)
Cod laksa (or Curried parsnip)

RENEW

5-day energizing cleanse

This cleanse is like a restorative tonic. Whether you are stressed out, finding it hard to jump out of bed in the morning, or feeling tired most of the time, a cleanse is a helpful way to replenish your reserves and renew your sense of vitality. In this cleanse, we have included a balance of calming foods that are described as "essence" foods in Chinese medicine.

Stress is one of the biggest challenges when it comes to sticking to healthy intentions. Kate remembers working on a book all about healthy eating and finding the deadlines so stress-inducing that her own diet and lifestyle went haywire. Stress is both physically and emotionally exhausting, so the last thing we want to do when we get home is to cook from scratch. It's easy to just pour a glass of wine, flop on the couch, and order a pizza. For this cleanse, clear your weekend so you have time to prepare some recipes for the days ahead.

Tips for the RENEW cleanse:

- Avoid processed or refined sugar.
- Avoid stimulants.
- Relax in the evenings and go to bed early.
- As soon as you wake in the morning, get out of bed.
- Meditation is ideal for this cleanse.
- Try an energizing movement exercise such as Qi Gong or Tai Chi or lots of gentle walking to get your "Qi" (vital force) flowing.

5-DAY RENEW MENU

PREPARE AHEAD
Roast chicken
Chicken stock (or Seaweed broth)
Bone broth (or Seaweed broth)
Bircher overnight oats (double batch)
Almond butter squash (double batch)
Beets and caraway (double batch)

DAY 1
Lemon juice and hot water
Dandelion tea
Bircher overnight oats
Sesame chicken (or Sprouted soup; double batch)
Asparagus mimosa

DAY 2
Lemon juice and hot water
Dandelion tea
Bircher overnight oats
Chicken and nettle tops (or Coconut chicken and kale or Sprouted soup)
Almond butter squash

DAY 3
Lemon juice and hot water
Nettle tea
Egg drop with nori
Almond butter squash
Bone broth (or Seaweed broth)
Beets and caraway

DAY 4
Lemon juice and hot water
Nettle tea
Berry kefir smoothie
Beets and caraway
Bone broth (or Seaweed broth)
Harissa broth with eggplant and quinoa (double batch)

DAY 5
Lemon juice and hot water
Dandelion tea
Avocado on rye toast
Harissa broth with eggplant and quinoa
Fennel-crusted salmon with ginger Chinese cabbage (or Green pho)

6

Recipes

Condiments, chutneys, and make-ahead garnishes

From a handful of radish sprouts to a spoonful of laksa paste or kimchi to a sprinkle of dukkah seeds, all these recipes offer instant flavor, texture, and added nutrition. They will add layers of flavor to your food.

Sprouts

People in cultures that consume grains, legumes, and seeds often sprout, or germinate, them to make them more digestible. Sprouting breaks down the antinutrients (compunds that reduce the body's ability to absorb nutrients) found in grains, legumes, and seeds to make the nutrients more bioavailable. The sprouting process itself boosts the nutrient profile of the grain, legume, or seed by increasing its vitamin content. Sprouting can also help people avoid the bloating and discomfort that some experience when eating these foods. We often sprout mung beans for a couple of days before making Kitchari (page 107) and love to add various sprouts to soups and salads as a garnish.

What you can sprout:

- Barley
- Spelt
- Lentils
- Green peas
- Mung beans
- Adzuki beans
- Chickpeas
- Alfalfa seeds

- Broccoli seeds
- Radish seeds
- Celery seeds
- Chica seeds
- Pumpkin seeds
- Sesame seeds
- Sunflower seeds

How to Sprout

Put the grains, legumes, or seeds in a bowl and add water to cover. Set aside on the counter to soak overnight. In the morning, drain in a colander and rinse with fresh water once or twice. Place the grains, legumes, or seeds in a sprouting jar (or mason jar) without any water and set it on its side. Screw on the mesh lid (or use cheesecloth secured with a rubber band) to allow the sprouts to breathe. Every morning and night, rinse the sprouts in the jar with fresh water, drain them, return them to the jar, put the lid or cloth back on, and set the jar on its side. The seeds should sprout within 1 to 4 days.

LAKSA PASTE

Laksa refers to a spicy noodle soup enjoyed in Southeast Asia. A spoonful of the laksa paste can be added to vegetable or chicken stock or spooned onto brown rice or noodles. It will keep for 1 month in an airtight container in the fridge.

170 calories

2 tablespoons coriander seeds

2 tablespoons cumin seeds

8 star anise pods

1 ounce red chile, seeded and chopped

1 (2-inch) piece fresh ginger, peeled and coarsely chopped

1 teaspoon ground galangal

15 kaffir lime leaves

7 lemongrass stalks

Toasted sesame oil, to blend

In a small skillet, toast the coriander, cumin, and star anise over medium heat just until they begin to release their aromas. Put the toasted spices on a plate to cool for a couple of minutes, then grind them in a spice grinder or using a mortar and pestle.

Place the ground spices and the remaining ingredients in a food processor and process until well combined, adding just enough sesame oil to blend the mixture into a smooth, but not runny, paste.

THAI PASTE

Lemongrass, hot peppers, lime, and ginger along with some other ingredients make a paste with the hallmark flavors of Thai food.

490 calories

1 or 2 fresh cayenne peppers, seeded and finely chopped

2 lemongrass stalks, finely chopped

1 (2-inch) piece fresh ginger, peeled and grated

Zest and juice of 2 limes

12 kaffir lime leaves

1 teaspoon coriander seeds

1 teaspoon cumin seeds

Put all the ingredients in a mortar and pestle or food processor and blend until smooth.

Store this homemade paste in an airtight container in the fridge for up to 1 month.

UMAMI MUSTARD

We found this sensational mustard called Anarchy in a Jar when we were visiting Brooklyn; it has the most incredible list of ingredients. Gather whatever ingredients you can and mix them together. You can make this mustard a few days ahead; it will keep in an airtight container in the refrigerator for up to 1 month.

Makes ¾ to 1 cup / 280 calories

¾ cup yellow mustard seeds (or brown, if you prefer hotter mustard)

⅔ cup apple cider vinegar

½ cup brewed matcha green tea, cooled, or water

¼ teaspoon nori flakes

1 tablespoon honey

½ teaspoon finely grated fresh ginger

¼ teaspoon smoked paprika

¼ teaspoon sea salt

In a bowl, combine the mustard seeds, vinegar, and matcha and soak for 48 hours. Pour the seeds and any remaining liquid into a food processor and add the nori, honey, ginger, paprika, and salt. Process to a paste.

CLEANSE SPICE MIX

Makes ¼ cup / 249 calories

1 tablespoon black mustard seeds

1 tablespoon cumin seeds

1 tablespoon fennel seeds

1 tablespoon black onion seeds

Mix all the ingredients together in a jar and store in a cool, dry place.

CLEANSE DUKKAH

Makes 6½ tablespoons / 340 calories

2 tablespoons sesame seeds

2 tablespoons pumpkin seeds

2 tablespoons hemp seeds

1 teaspoon nori flakes

½ teaspoon ground turmeric

Mix all the ingredients together in a jar and store in a cool, dry place.

KIMCHI

This recipe, a cross between Korean kimchi and sauerkraut, is adapted from a white kimchi recipe we came across in *Bon Appétit* magazine.

42 calories

1 (1½-inch) piece fresh ginger, peeled

3 garlic cloves

2 tablespoons sea salt

1 small head cabbage (about 1 pound), shredded

½ daikon, peeled and thinly sliced

4 scallions, thinly sliced

Put the ginger, garlic, and salt in a food processor or mortar and pestle and process or grind to a paste.

Combine the paste and all the vegetables in a large bowl and massage with your hands until the mixture is thoroughly combined and the cabbage begins to release its juices. As you continue, more liquid will be released until there is enough to cover the cabbage when it is pressed down.

Transfer the cabbage and all the liquid to a glass jar. Make sure the cabbage is submerged, then cover the mouth of the jar with cheesecloth and secure it with a rubber band.

Allow the kimchi to ferment for 5 days at room temperature. Remove the cheesecloth, put a lid on the jar, and refrigerate up to 6 months.

SAFFRON YOGURT

Since saffron is said to be the most expensive spice in the world, making yogurt with it may seem like a bit of a luxury, but a little bit goes a long way. Treating yourself is vital, and this is both beautiful and a delicate, delicious taste that makes a change from plain yogurt.

Makes about 1 cup / 194 calories

Small pinch of saffron threads

3 tablespoons boiling water

¾ cup plain Greek yogurt

2 tablespoons lemon juice

1 tablespoon extra-virgin olive oil

In a small bowl, soak the saffron threads in the boiling water for 10 minutes.

Add the yogurt, lemon juice, and olive oil and stir to combine. Transfer to an airtight container and refrigerate for up to 3 days.

Infused Oils

Nicole loves to add flavors to olive oil and see what happens—a favorite is an infusion of nori flakes. We also love a combination of cardamom and garlic cloves, or adding a few sprigs of rosemary to a bottle and waiting a week or so. These oils are perfect for adding a swirl of extra flavor to your soups.

Stocks and Broths

Sundays are ideal for making stocks. Put a pot on the stove and go about your day; your house will soon smell great.

ROAST CHICKEN AND BROWN CHICKEN STOCK

This method of roasting a chicken is inspired by the Chinese method of cooking pork belly. But do feel free to use your favorite recipe and then make your stock with the carcass.

---

130 calories

---

1 (2½- to 3-pound) whole chicken

1 lemon, halved

A few rosemary sprigs

Sea salt

1 onion, coarsely chopped

1 leek, sliced

2 bay leaves

1 tablespoon tomato paste

1 small bunch fresh tarragon

Preheat the oven to 425°F. Poke the chicken with a skewer all over to create small holes in the skin. Place the chicken in the sink and pour a kettle of boiling water over it. (This helps give the chicken a crispy skin without overcooking the meat). Let the chicken drain, then pat it dry and set it in a roasting pan. Rub the lemon halves over its skin, then place them in the cavity and add the rosemary sprigs. Sprinkle the skin with sea salt.

Roast the chicken for 10 minutes, then lower the oven temperature to 375°F and cook until a meat thermometer inserted into the thickest part of the thigh registers 165°F. When the chicken is cooked, let it rest until it is cool enough to handle. Remove the meat from the chicken and reserve the carcass. Use the meat immediately or freeze it for another recipe.

To make the stock, preheat the oven to 375°F. Put the chicken carcass in a Dutch oven and add cold water to cover. Bring the water to a boil, uncovered, then transfer the Dutch oven to the oven and cook for 4 hours.

Leave the oven on, but transfer the Dutch oven to the stovetop over high heat. Add the onion, leek, bay leaves, and tomato paste. Bring to a boil, then return the pot to the oven for 1 hour. After 1 hour, add the tarragon, turn off the oven, and allow to rest inside the oven for 30 minutes.

Strain the stock through a colander, discarding all the solids. Once cool, transfer the stock to an airtight container and refrigerate for 3 to 4 days or freeze for up to 1 month.

SEAWEED BROTH

This makes an excellent base for fish soups or an alternative to vegetable stock. Enjoy a cup by itself.

Makes 1 quart / 49 calories

2 sheets kombu

1 celery stalk, coarsely chopped

1 onion, coarsely chopped

1 teaspoon black peppercorns

1 teaspoon capers, rinsed

Put all the ingredients in a stockpot and add 1 quart water. Bring to a boil over high heat, then reduce the heat to maintain a simmer and cook for 45 minutes. Strain through a colander, discarding all the solids. Let cool, then transfer the broth to an airtight container. Refrigerate for up to 1 week or freeze for up to 1 month.

TURMERIC, GINGER, AND LEMONGRASS BROTH

Turmeric is among the most powerful natural anti-inflammatory ingredients known at present. It needs to be mixed with black pepper to be assimilated into the body for greatest effect. Ginger is also an anti-inflammatory, as well as an antioxidant.

Makes 1 quart / 30 calories

2 lemongrass stalks, smashed

1 teaspoon grated fresh turmeric

2 teaspoons grated fresh ginger

Juice of 1 lemon

Freshly ground black pepper

Put the lemongrass and 1 quart water in a saucepan. Bring to a boil over high heat, then reduce the heat to maintain a simmer and cook for 10 minutes. Stir in the turmeric, ginger, lemon, and some black pepper and simmer for 3 minutes. Let the broth cool, then strain through a colander, discarding all the solids. Once cool, transfer the broth to an airtight container. Drink the broth warm or chilled, in small amounts. It will keep in the refrigerator for up to 1 week or in the freezer for up to 1 month.

BONE BROTH

Bone broth can be enjoyed on its own or used to flavor many other dishes. Use good-quality pastured meat.

Makes 1 quart / 220 calories

2 pounds veal or beef marrow bones

1 pound beef shins or necks

1 pound chicken necks, wings, or backs

1 onion, quartered

1 leek, halved and sliced

1 celery stalk, coarsely chopped

1 garlic clove

Preheat the oven to 425°F. Place the bones and chicken in a roasting pan and roast for 40 minutes. Transfer the bones and chicken to a stockpot. Add the remaining ingredients and enough water to cover the meat and bones by 3 inches. Bring to a boil, then reduce the heat to maintain a simmer. Cook very slowly for up to 8 hours, scooping off any scum that rises to the surface and checking to make sure the bones and chicken are covered by the liquid. The broth will become quite thick and gelatinous.

Strain the broth through a sieve lined with cheesecloth, discarding all the solids. Let cool, then transfer the broth to an airtight container. It will keep in the refrigerator for up to 1 week or in the freezer for up to 1 month. Depending on how concentrated the broth is, you can dilute it with water as desired when you use it.

VEGETABLE STOCK

This makes a delicate, aromatic vegetable stock, perfect for the cleanse recipes.

Makes 1 quart / 78 calories

1 leek, coarsely chopped

1 white onion, coarsely chopped

½ small celeriac, coarsely chopped

1 celery stalk, coarsely chopped

1 fennel bulb, coarsely chopped

6 garlic cloves, smashed

1 teaspoon coriander seeds

Sea salt

Handful of mixed fresh herbs, such as parsley, dill, cilantro, and tarragon

Combine the vegetables, garlic, coriander seeds, and a little salt in a stockpot and add 1½ quarts water. Bring to a boil over high heat, then reduce the heat to maintain a simmer and cook for 45 minutes, until the vegetables have softened. Turn off the heat and add the herbs. Let cool, then strain the stock through a colander and discard all the solids.

Transfer the stock to an airtight container. It will keep in the refrigerator for up to 1 week or in the freezer for up to 1 month.

Breakfast

OVERNIGHT OATS

It isn't always easy to eat a good breakfast when you're rushing to work or trying to get the kids out the door. This recipe for overnight oats is so versatile because they soak overnight while you sleep. They'll be ready to cook first thing in the morning. You can add all kinds of toppings. Soaking oats makes them easier to digest, which is good news when you're trying to give your body a chance to rest and restore.

The oats will keep in the refrigerator in an airtight container for up to 3 days, so you can triple the recipe.

Serves 1 / 221 calories

½ cup rolled oats (use gluten-free if you are intolerant)

1 teaspoon flaxseed meal

1 teaspoon chia seeds

1 teaspoon sesame seeds

Pinch of ground cinnamon

⅔ cup almond or coconut milk (or coconut water, if you prefer)

Few drops of pure vanilla extract

In a glass jar, combine the oats, seeds, and cinnamon, then add the almond milk and the vanilla. Stir thoroughly to combine. Cover and refrigerate overnight.

Toppings

CLOVE-SPICED APPLE

165 calories

Heat your oats with a little more water or nut milk in a saucepan. Heat a little coconut oil in a skillet and add about 6 whole cloves. Once the cloves release their aroma, remove them from the oil. Add chopped apple pieces and some almonds to the skillet. Once the apples start to brown, spoon the mixture on top of the oats.

BIRCHER

152 calories

Bircher muesli is served cold, so it's easy to prepare first thing. When you are ready to serve the oats, stir in the juice of ½ lime and a few drops of pure vanilla extract, a few chopped hazelnuts, a chopped apple or pear, and a couple spoonfuls of plain Greek yogurt, if you like.

BERRY COMPOTE

59 calories

Combine some frozen berries (blueberries, raspberries, blackberries) in a saucepan with a little water and a drizzle of honey and heat until the berries begin to break down and reduce. Use warm or transfer to an airtight jar and refrigerate for up to 1 week. To serve with the overnight oats, heat the oats in a pan with a little extra nondairy milk and top with the compote and a spoonful of plain Greek yogurt, if you like.

EGG DROP SOUP WITH NORI

When you have extra time for breakfast, this is a lovely way to enjoy eggs without the usual slice of toast. Many Asian cultures start the day with a bowl of savory broth or soup instead of sweetened cereals or baked goods.

Serves 1 / 330 calories

1 teaspoon white miso paste, or 1 package dried miso soup mix

1 teaspoon nori flakes

2 large eggs, beaten

Sea salt and freshly ground black pepper

1 spring onion, finely sliced

1 teaspoon toasted sesame oil

In a small saucepan, bring 1¼ cups water to a boil (alternatively, use as much water as the miso soup packet indicates). Add the miso paste and stir to dissolve. Reduce the heat to maintain a simmer. Stir in the nori flakes. Slowly pour the eggs into the soup in a thin stream, stirring gently, to create ribbons as the eggs cook. Remove from the heat. Taste and adjust the seasoning.

Sprinkle on the chopped onion and drizzle with the sesame oil before serving.

MISO BREAKFAST BROTH

This is another savory breakfast option to fire up your energy in the morning. You can prepare this the night before by cooking the quinoa and buckwheat and making the broth without adding the tofu. In the morning, heat up the miso, seaweed, and grains and add the tofu just before serving.

Serves 1 / 148 calories

2 tablespoons quinoa

¼ cup buckwheat groats (kasha)

½ teaspoon brown miso paste

A few strips of wakame, soaked and cut into 1½-inch pieces

2½ ounces firm tofu, cut into cubes

½ teaspoon black or white sesame seeds

Bring a saucepan of water to a boil. Add the quinoa and groats and simmer for 15 minutes. Drain the grains through a sieve and set aside.

In a small saucepan, bring 1¼ cups water to a boil. Add the miso paste and stir to dissolve. Reduce the heat to maintain a simmer. Add the grains, wakame, and tofu to the miso and heat through. Pour into a bowl and sprinkle with the sesame seeds before serving.

Smoothies

The great thing about blending up a smoothie is that you can pack it with healthy ingredients and take it on the go with you. Berries (blueberries, açai paste, raspberries, blackberries) are our favorite fruits, so we love to combine them with kefir for a boost. The Almond Chia and Avocado Nuts smoothies are particularly good for vegetarians, or if you are having a meat-free day, as they contain both protein and good fats.

BERRY KEFIR BOOSTER

146 calories

1 cup frozen blueberries

½ cup kefir

Unsweetened almond milk

2 or 3 drops pure vanilla extract (optional)

Flaxseed meal (optional)

In a blender, combine and blend until smooth. Add the vanilla, if desired, for extra sweetness. You can also add a tablespoon of flaxseed meal for extra fiber.

Note: Kefir is fermented and contains lots of beneficial bacteria. It's like yogurt, so if you can't find it, use plain Greek yogurt instead.

ALMOND CHIA

Serves 1 / 312 calories

1 tablespoon almond butter

2 tablespoons plain Greek yogurt

1 tablespoon soaked chia seeds (1 teaspoon dry seeds soaked in ¼ cup water overnight)

½ frozen banana, or 3 tablespoons frozen blueberries

½ cup coconut milk

Blend all the ingredients together until smooth.

AVOCADO NUTS

Serves 2 / 271 calories

1 avocado, pitted and peeled

1 cup almond milk

1 tablespoon almond butter

1 teaspoon flaxseed oil

1 teaspoon agave syrup

1 teaspoon grated fresh ginger

2 or 3 ice cubes

Blend all the ingredients until well combined.

Snacks

NOURISH BITES

These confections are perfect to have on hand for any time you need a bit of nourishment or after a workout.

Makes 10 / 150 calories

½ cup almonds

2 tablespoons hemp seeds

4 ounces dried apple rings

1 teaspoon spirulina

1 teaspoon açai powder

2 tablespoons coconut oil

⅓ cup unsweetened shredded coconut

2 tablespoons honey

1 tablespoon sesame seeds, for rolling

Combine all the ingredients, except the sesame seeds, in a food processor and process into a paste. Divide the mixture into 10 pieces. Roll each piece into a ball. Roll each ball in the sesame seeds to coat. Refrigerate in an airtight container for up to 5 days.

KALE CHIPS

Kate loves crunchy chips, and these bites of kale satisfy her cravings.

Makes 4 servings / 225 calories

4 ounces shredded kale leaves

1 tablespoon extra-virgin olive oil

Sea salt

1 tablespoon pumpkin seeds

Preheat the oven to 275°F. In a large bowl, toss the kale with the olive oil and a good pinch of salt. Arrange on a baking sheet and bake for 20 minutes, tossing with tongs after 10 minutes, until the kale is crispy. Stir in the pumpkin seeds during the last 5 minutes to toast.

TURMERIC AND BLACK PEPPER OATCAKES

You can add different flavors to homemade oatcakes, such as dried herbs, paprika, and other spices. One of our favorite combinations is turmeric and black pepper, and these make the perfect accompaniment to all our vegetarian soups.

Makes about 20 / 51 calories

2½ cups rolled oats

1 tablespoon extra-virgin olive oil

¼ teaspoon ground turmeric

Good pinch of freshly ground black pepper

¼ teaspoon sea salt

½ cup boiling water

Preheat the oven to 350°F. Put the oats in a large bowl. Add the olive oil, turmeric, pepper, and salt to taste and mix. Add the boiling water and ½ cup cold water and stir until the mixture comes together. (If you add too much water, just add some more oats.) Shape the mixture into balls, then press them into flat ¼-inch-thick pieces. Using a knife, score the tops of the pieces. Use a spatula to lift the pieces onto a baking sheet. Bake for 20 to 30 minutes, depending on their thickness, until golden.

Drinks

Drinking plenty of water throughout the day is one of the best things you can do for your digestion. The only time when it is best not to drink a lot of water is while you are eating, so as not to flood the digestive system at the same time that it is handling food.

First thing in the morning, sip hot water with a squeeze of lemon. You can add some fresh mint, too.

The best cleansing teas include:
- Fennel
- Nettle
- Dandelion
- Green
- Fresh mint

Green tea is a powerful antioxidant and activates enzymes in the liver that help eliminate toxins from the body. It needs to be steeped for 5 to 10 minutes to release its beneficial catechins.

Many people find it helps to drink a glass of water with a capful of apple cider vinegar added every day.

Look for kombucha in your local health food store. Kombucha is a tangy, fermented drink that contains beneficial bacteria.

Naturally flavored waters:
- Strips of cucumber and crushed fresh mint leaves
- Lemon and lime

Naturally flavored coconut water:
Coconut water is packed with potassium and is naturally isotonic, helping your body to rehydrate itself, particularly after exercise. Add:
- Melon juice
- Cucumber and fresh mint

And for a hot, health-boosting drink, add a little turmeric, lemon juice, fresh grated ginger, and honey to hot water.

Soups

RESOLVE

AVOCADO, LEMON, TURMERIC, AND CAYENNE

Avocados are high in heart-healthy monounsaturated fats (MUFAs) and fiber, and they make us feel full longer.

Serves 1 / 163 calories

½ **ripe Hass avocado, pitted and peeled**

½ **cup coconut milk**

Pinch of sea salt

Pinch of cayenne pepper

¼ **teaspoon ground turmeric**

Pinch of freshly ground black pepper

Zest and juice of ½ small lemon

Scoop the flesh of the avocado into a blender. Add half the coconut milk and blend until smooth. Add the rest of the coconut milk in stages until you reach the desired consistency.

Add the salt, cayenne pepper, turmeric, black pepper, lemon zest, and lemon juice and blend again. Taste to check the flavor, and if you are happy with it, pour the soup into a container. Squeeze a bit more lemon juice over the top and press a piece of parchment paper directly against the surface of the soup (to avoid exposure to the air and reduce discoloration).

Chill in the refrigerator before serving. If you want to serve the soup immediately, add a couple of ice cubes when blending to chill it.

CORN, KALE, AND AVOCADO

Coconut and chile give the perfect punch to this combo. As part of the cruciferous family, kale is a rich source of antioxidants and has anti-inflammatory properties. Steaming kale is thought to maximize its nutritional benefits.

Serves 2 / 230 calories

1 ear corn, or ½ cup frozen corn kernels

3 cups chopped kale

1 tablespoon coconut oil

½ teaspoon red pepper flakes

1¾ cups hot vegetable or chicken stock (pages 75 and 70)

1 medium Hass avocado, pitted, peeled, and sliced, for serving

Bring a saucepan of water to a boil. Add the ear of corn and cook for 3 to 6 minutes. Drain and let cool, then slice off the kernels with a knife. (Skip this step if using frozen corn.)

While the corn is cooking, put 1 cup water in a skillet and bring to a boil. Add the kale, cover, and steam for 5 minutes.

Heat the coconut oil in a Dutch oven and add the corn kernels and red pepper flakes. Cook for a couple of minutes, then add the kale and cook for 3 to 4 minutes more. Add the hot stock and bring to a boil, then reduce the heat to maintain a simmer and cook for a minute to bring the flavors together. Taste and adjust the seasoning. Ladle the soup into bowls and top with the avocado slices.

BALTI-SPICED CAULIFLOWER

Balti is a blend of spices used in Indian cooking. Spices can be great for nourishing the digestive system. Adding them to your cooking is an easy way to improve your diet.

Serves 2 / 214 calories

For the Balti Spice

1 teaspoon cumin seeds

1 teaspoon coriander seeds

½ teaspoon fenugreek seeds

¼ teaspoon red pepper flakes

½ teaspoon ground turmeric

1 teaspoon paprika

For the Soup

2 tablespoons extra-virgin olive oil

1 small or ½ large cauliflower (about 1 pound), cut into small florets

1 cup hot vegetable or chicken stock (pages 75 and 70)

Saffron Yogurt (page 68)

To make the Balti spice, in a small skillet, toast the cumin, coriander, and fenugreek seeds over medium heat until they become fragrant. Take care not to burn them. Combine the toasted seeds and red pepper flakes in a spice grinder or a mortar and pestle. Mix with the ground turmeric and paprika. Transfer to an airtight jar and store at room temperature in a cool, dark place for months. Use with other soups and vegetables.

To make the soup, heat the olive oil in a stockpot. Add 1 teaspoon of the Balti spice. As the aromas are released, after about 30 seconds, add the cauliflower and stir to coat with the spiced oil. Sauté the cauliflower for 2 to 3 minutes before adding the hot stock. Bring to a boil, then reduce the heat. Pierce the cauliflower with a knife; it should be cooked, but not soft. Remove from the heat.

To serve, ladle the soup into bowls and top each with a spoonful of saffron yogurt.

BEETS, COCONUT, AND SALMON

Herbalists call beets the vitality plant—they are nourishing and contain antioxidants, magnesium, and iron; few calories; and lots of fiber. Salmon is a powerful source of healthy omega-3 essential fatty acids and protein, so a bowl of this soup is packed with good nutrition.

Serves 2 / 307 calories

1 bay leaf

6 black peppercorns

1 (6- to 8-ounce) skin-on salmon fillet

2 teaspoons coconut oil, plus more if needed

1 small red onion, diced

1 (½-inch) piece fresh ginger, peeled and finely chopped

1 garlic clove, finely chopped

½ pound beets, peeled and coarsely chopped

1 cup hot vegetable stock (page 75)

1⅔ cups canned light coconut milk

To poach the salmon, combine 2 cups water, the bay leaf, and the peppercorns in a wide saucepan. Bring to a boil. Add the salmon, cover the saucepan, and turn off the heat. Let the salmon sit in the hot water for 8 to 10 minutes. Pierce with a knife to make sure it is cooked through. Transfer the salmon to a plate and use a fork to flake the fish into bite-size pieces.

Heat the coconut oil in a Dutch oven. Add the onion and sauté until soft, about 5 minutes. Add the ginger and garlic. Add the beets to the pan and cook for 5 minutes more, then add the hot stock. Bring to a boil, then reduce the heat to maintain a simmer and cook until the beets can be easily pierced with a knife.

Add the coconut milk to the soup and simmer for 5 minutes more. Blend the soup directly in the pot with an immersion blender or transfer to a food processor and process until smooth.

Pour the soup into bowls and stir in the flaked salmon.

CHICKEN SOUP FOR THE CLEANSED SOUL

The combination of slow-cooked chicken with stock and spices (for your digestion) with the fresh peas and crunchy bean sprouts and napa cabbage (antioxidant and anti-inflammatory) works really well.

Serves 2 / 286 calories

½ teaspoon ground turmeric

1 teaspoon fennel seeds

Pinch of red pepper flakes

1 tablespoon peanut oil

2 large bone-in chicken thighs

Hot chicken stock, as needed (page 70)

2 garlic cloves, smashed

A few curry leaves

2 bay leaves

A few strips of lemon zest

⅓ cup fresh or frozen peas

½ cup fresh bean sprouts, rinsed

½ cup shredded napa cabbage

Combine the turmeric, fennel seeds, red pepper flakes, and peanut oil in a large bowl. Add the chicken pieces to the spice mix and toss well to coat.

Heat a Dutch oven over medium-high heat. Sear the chicken thighs on both sides, then add the hot stock, garlic, curry leaves, bay leaves, and lemon zest. Simmer gently, uncovered, until the meat easily separates from the bones, 45 minutes to 1 hour.

Remove the chicken from the stock and let cool. When cool enough to handle, shred the meat. Return the shredded chicken to the stock, along with the fresh peas, bean sprouts, and cabbage and heat through. Divide the soup between two bowls.

CURRIED PARSNIP AND APPLE

A naturally sweet and comforting soup for the colder months. Coconut milk is the perfect alternative to cream. Root vegetables are a rich source of fiber and easy on the digestion. It's good to remember that they draw their nutrients from the soil, reminding us of the importance of taking care of the earth.

Serves 2 / 277 calories

1 tablespoon extra-virgin olive oil

1 large parsnip, scrubbed if organic, peeled if not, and coarsely chopped

1 teaspoon garam masala

1 cup hot vegetable stock (page 75)

½ cup coconut milk

Sea salt and freshly ground black pepper

1 tablespoon coconut oil

1 apple, cored and sliced, for serving

Heat the olive oil in a Dutch oven. Add the parsnip and sauté until it begins to turn brown. Push the parsnip to the sides to create a space on the bottom of the pan and add the garam masala. Cook for about 30 seconds, until the spices become fragrant, then stir in the parsnip. Add the hot stock and some boiling water, if needed, to cover the parsnip. Bring to a boil, then reduce the heat to maintain a simmer and cook for about 15 minutes. Add the coconut milk, return to a simmer, and cook until the parsnip is soft, about 30 minutes.

Allow the soup to cool a little, then blend the soup directly in the pot with an immersion blender or transfer to a food processor and process until smooth. Taste and adjust the seasoning.

Heat the coconut oil in a skillet. Add the apples and sauté until golden.

To serve, divide the soup between two bowls and arrange the apple slices on top of the soup.

GREEN GAZPACHO

This chilled green soup is perfect for a hot summer's day.

Serves 2 / 199 calories

4 ounces baby spinach

½ cucumber, peeled, seeded, and chopped

Small handful of fresh basil leaves

Small handful of fresh mint leaves

½ avocado, pitted and peeled

Pinch of cayenne pepper

½ cup plain Greek yogurt or kefir

1 tablespoon apple cider vinegar

Sea salt and freshly ground black pepper

1 tablespoon extra-virgin olive oil

2 breakfast radishes, thinly sliced, for serving

Radish sprouts, for serving

In a food processor, combine the spinach, cucumber, basil, mint, avocado, cayenne, yogurt, and vinegar and process until smooth. You may need to add a little water to reach the desired consistency. Taste and adjust the seasoning.

To serve, divide the soup between two bowls and drizzle with the olive oil. Sprinkle the radish slices and sprouts over the top.

HOT CUCUMBER WITH SALMON

Salmon and cucumber are a classic combination. Cucumber, known for its diuretic properties, helps the body get rid of excess water. It is naturally hydrating and the skin is full of fiber.

Serves 2 / 275 calories

1¼ cups chicken stock (page 70)

1¼ cups vegetable stock (page 75)

1 lemongrass stalk, smashed

1 (4- to 6-ounce) skinless salmon fillet

1 small cucumber, seeded and sliced

3 scallions, sliced

1 tablespoon tamari (wheat-free soy sauce)

1 (1-inch) piece fresh ginger, peeled and thinly sliced, for serving

Combine the chicken stock and vegetable stock in a saucepan and bring to a boil. Reduce the heat to maintain a simmer and add the lemongrass. Simmer for 10 minutes.

Set a steamer rack over the simmering stock and set the salmon in the steamer. Steam for 3 minutes, then remove from the heat and keep the salmon in the covered steamer for 5 minutes more.

Using a slotted spoon, remove the lemongrass from the stock, then add the cucumber, scallions, and tamari. Flake the salmon into bowls, pour in the aromatic soup, and serve with fresh ginger slices scattered over the top.

HOT CUCUMBER WITH BARLEY

The barley helps eliminate water retention, so this soup is perfect for when you feel bloated.

Serves 2 / 206 calories

2½ cups vegetable stock (page 75)

1 lemongrass stalk, smashed

⅓ cup pearl barley

1 small cucumber, seeded and sliced

3 scallions, sliced

1 Thai chile, thinly sliced

1 tablespoon tamari (wheat-free soy sauce)

1 (1-inch) piece fresh ginger, peeled and thinly sliced, for serving

Bring the stock to a boil in a Dutch oven, then reduce the heat to maintain a simmer. Add the lemongrass and barley. Cover, leaving a bit of a gap between the lid and pan so the stock doesn't boil over. Once the barley is tender, about 45 minutes, take the pan off the heat and remove the lemongrass.

Stir in the cucumber, scallions, chile, and soy sauce. Divide the soup between two bowls and serve with fresh ginger slices scattered on top.

LEEK, FENNEL, AND CELERY WITH RED LENTILS

The vegetables in this soup have diuretic properties that help eliminate excess water in the body, or "damp," as Chinese medicine aptly describes it.

Serves 2 / 237 calories

1 tablespoon extra-virgin olive oil

1 leek, finely chopped

1 celery heart (keep the outer stalks for stock), cut into small pieces

Inner leaves of 1 fennel bulb (keep the outer part for stock), cut into small pieces

1 cup hot vegetable stock (page 75)

¾ cup red lentils, rinsed

½ preserved lemon, finely chopped

2 slices rye toast, for serving

Heat the olive oil in a Dutch oven over medium heat. Add the leek, celery, and fennel and sauté until soft, 10 to 12 minutes.

Add the hot stock and lentils, bring to a boil, then reduce the heat to maintain a simmer and cook for about 20 minutes. Add the preserved lemon, stir to combine, then remove the pot from the heat. Ideally, allow the soup to sit overnight, as it improves as the flavors infuse.

To serve, reheat and accompany with a slice of rye toast.

SOUTH INDIAN MAHI MAHI WITH SEA BEANS

You can use any firm white-fleshed fish, such as cod, for this recipe. Seashore nutrition is returning to our cooking and we have used sea beans here, grown on marshes close to the sea and containing phytochemicals that are protective of the liver.

Serves 2 / 349 calories

1 tablespoon coconut oil

1 (1½-inch) cinnamon stick

4 whole cloves

½ teaspoon mustard seeds

8 curry leaves

½ onion, thinly sliced

2 garlic cloves, crushed

1 teaspoon grated fresh ginger

½ teaspoon ground turmeric, or ¼ teaspoon grated fresh turmeric

½ cup vegetable stock (page 75)

½ cup coconut milk

3 ounces sea beans, rinsed

6 ounces mahi mahi or other firm white-fleshed fish

½ teaspoon white miso paste

½ lime, for serving

Heat half the coconut oil in a Dutch oven. Add the cinnamon, cloves, mustard seeds, and curry leaves. When the aromas are released and the mustard seeds are just starting to pop, add the onion and sauté for 8 to 10 minutes before adding the garlic, ginger, and turmeric.

Meanwhile, bring the stock and coconut milk to a boil in a separate pan, then reduce the heat to a simmer. Pour the hot stock and coconut milk into the pan with the onions.

Heat the remaining coconut oil in a skillet. Add the sea beans and sauté for a few minutes, then remove from the pan. Brush the fish fillets with the white miso and fry, skin side down, in the skillet for about 5 minutes, until almost cooked through. Turn them over and remove the pan from the heat. The fillets will finish cooking in the residual heat. Use a fork to flake the fish.

To serve, divide the coconut broth between two bowls, stir in the flaked fish, and sprinkle with the sea beans. Squeeze lime juice on top before serving.

SALMON POACHED IN LEMONGRASS TEA

This soup's clean flavors come from the refreshing lemongrass, celery, and peppery radishes.

Serves 2 / 309 calories

1 quart hot lemongrass tea

1 (4-ounce) skin-on salmon fillet

1 celery stalk, cut into 1-inch pieces

Small handful of radishes, thinly sliced

Furikake or a mixture of black and white sesame seeds

Sea salt and freshly ground black pepper

Bring half the tea to a boil in a saucepan and add the salmon. Reduce the heat to maintain a simmer and poach for about 8 minutes, or until the flesh can be flaked with a fork. Remove the salmon and flake the flesh, discarding the skin.

Divide the celery and radishes between two serving bowls, add the salmon flakes, then pour over the remaining hot tea. Season with furikake and salt and pepper, then serve.

SUMMER CHICKEN

This is a delicious way to enjoy fresh summer vegetables, all the flavors brought together in a little warming broth. If using fresh fava beans, they will need to be removed from their pods, blanched, and then peeled as directed.

Serves 2 / 268 calories

- ⅓ cup fresh (about 2 ounces in the pods) or frozen fava or lima beans
- 1¾ cups chicken stock (page 70)
- 1 cup shredded cooked chicken (reserved from making stock)
- Small handful of fresh mint leaves, shredded
- ⅓ cup fresh or frozen peas
- 1 small head Boston lettuce, shredded
- 2 tablespoons plain Greek yogurt, for serving

If using fresh fava beans, remove them from their pods. Bring 2 cups water to a boil in a saucepan. Add the beans, blanch them for 30 seconds, drain them, and immediately plunge them into a bowl of ice water to stop the cooking. Using your thumb and forefinger, pop off and discard the waxy coating around each bean.

Bring the chicken stock to a boil in a saucepan, then reduce the heat to maintain a simmer. Add the chicken, mint, fava beans, and peas and cook just to heat through, a minute or so. Taste and adjust the seasoning, ladle into bowls, and top with the lettuce and yogurt.

WILD GARLIC, BABY SPINACH, AND OLIVES

Garlic, with its many sulfur compounds, helps to clear the inside of the digestive tract. It detoxifies the gut from pathogens and at the same time supports "good" bacteria. Look for wild garlic, or garlic leaves, at farmers' markets in the spring.

Serves 2 / 211 calories

¼ cup brown rice

1 tablespoon extra-virgin olive oil

2 shallots, finely sliced

1.75 ounces wild garlic, coarsely chopped

2 ounces baby spinach

¼ cup kalamata olives, pitted and sliced

2 cups chicken or vegetable stock (pages 70 and 75)

Combine the rice and 1 cup water in a saucepan and bring to a boil. Reduce the heat to low, cover, and simmer until the liquid has been absorbed, 30 to 35 minutes. Let stand, covered, for 5 minutes, then fluff with a fork.

Meanwhile, heat the olive oil in a large skillet, add the shallots, and sauté for a few minutes, until soft. Add in the wild garlic and cook for a couple of minutes, then add the spinach and olives. Stir well and cook until the spinach is just wilted.

Meanwhile, heat the stock in a saucepan. Divide the cooked rice between two bowls and top with the wild garlic, spinach, and olives, then ladle in the hot stock.

REDUCE AND REBALANCE

ASPARAGUS MIMOSA

This soup is seasonal, perfect for late spring. Asparagus contains a number of anti-inflammatory nutrients, and like Jerusalem artichokes has prebiotic properties, making it supportive to digestive health.

Serves 2 / 241 calories

1 large egg

¼ celery stalk, finely chopped

Sea salt

½ pound asparagus

1 tablespoon extra-virgin olive oil

2 cups hot vegetable or chicken stock (pages 75 and 70)

2 tablespoons plain Greek yogurt

Place the egg in a saucepan and add water to cover. Bring the water to a boil and cook the egg for 8 minutes from the point that the water boils. Remove from the water with a slotted spoon and cool under running water, then peel and chop. In a bowl, mix the egg with the celery, then season with a pinch of sea salt.

Snap off the woody parts of the asparagus (keep them for making stock) and chop the spears into 1-inch pieces.

Heat the oil in a saucepan, add the asparagus, and sauté for 2 minutes before adding enough stock to cover. Bring to a boil, then reduce the heat to maintain a simmer and cook until the asparagus are tender, which should only take a few minutes. Remove the asparagus pieces using a slotted spoon and transfer to a blender. Blend until smooth, then taste and adjust the seasoning.

Stir the yogurt into the blended asparagus and divide the mixture between two bowls. Serve with the chopped egg and celery scattered on top.

CHICKEN AND ZUCCHINI THAI NOODLE SOUP

Zucchini are plentiful in late summer and are a good source of antioxidants in the form of carotenoids.

Serves 2 / 383 calories

1 tablespoon coconut oil

1 tablespoon Thai Paste (page 64)

1 large or 2 small carrots, grated

3 cups chicken stock (page 70)

1 cup coconut milk

1 cup shredded cooked chicken (reserved from making stock)

1 zucchini, shaved into long, thin "noodles" with a vegetable peeler

Small handful of fresh Thai basil leaves, for serving

Heat the coconut oil in a large saucepan. Stir in the Thai Paste and, a few seconds later, add the grated carrot and stir well. After a minute or so, add the stock and coconut milk, bring to a boil, then reduce the heat to maintain a simmer.

Add the chicken and zucchini ribbons and warm through. Remove from the heat and let the flavors infuse for a couple of minutes before serving in deep bowls, with Thai basil scattered on top.

COCONUT CHICKEN WITH TURMERIC AND KALE

If kale isn't available, use another dark, leafy green like collards or mustard.

Serves 1 / 378 calories

½ small onion, chopped

1 tablespoon coconut oil, melted

½ cup unsweetened coconut water

1 teaspoon ground turmeric, or ¼ teaspoon grated fresh turmeric

Freshly ground black pepper

2 to 3 ounces shredded kale leaves

1½ teaspoons pumpkin seeds

½ cup shredded cooked chicken (reserved from making stock)

Squeeze of lemon juice (optional)

In a skillet, sauté the onion in ½ tablespoon of the coconut oil until soft. Add the coconut water, turmeric, and some freshly ground black pepper. Transfer the cooked onion to a bowl.

Heat the remaining ½ tablespoon oil in a skillet. Add the kale and sauté for a few minutes until slightly softened. Stir in the pumpkin seeds.

Place the kale and shredded chicken in a bowl and add the hot coconut water. Taste it—it might need a squeeze of lemon.

ZUCCHINI, LEMON, AND THYME

In our soup cookbook, *Magic Soup*, we made zucchini and za'atar soup. There many variations of za'atar, a Middle Eastern spice blend, usually made with thyme, sumac, and sesame seeds.

Serves 2 / 188 calories

2 tablespoons extra-virgin olive oil

3 or 4 medium zucchini, cut into cubes

1 teaspoon fresh thyme leaves, finely chopped

Zest of ½ lemon

1¼ cups hot chicken or vegetable stock (pages 70 and 75)

1 tablespoon pumpkin seeds

Heat the olive oil in a saucepan. Add the zucchini and sauté for 3 minutes. Stir in the thyme and half the lemon zest.

Add the hot stock, bring to a boil, then reduce the heat to maintain a simmer and cook gently until the zucchini is tender but not too soft.

In the meantime, heat a skillet and toast the pumpkin seeds with the remainder of the lemon zest until they just begin to pop a little—keep shaking the pan to prevent them from burning.

Remove the zucchini from the heat and let cool, then transfer half to a food processor with as much stock from the pan as necessary to achieve the desired consistency (you may prefer a smoother or chunkier soup).

Divide the remaining zucchini between two bowls, creating a pyramid in the middle. Ladle the blended soup around the zucchini and sprinkle with the toasted pumpkin seeds.

FIVE-SPICE TOFU

Tofu is a good source of vegetarian protein and takes on any spice or herb flavors that you like.

Serves 2 / 146 calories

1 cup cubed firm tofu (1-inch cubes)

½ teaspoon mustard seeds, crushed

½ teaspoon black onion seeds, crushed

¼ teaspoon sea salt

½ teaspoon Chinese five-spice powder

1 teaspoon white miso paste

1 tablespoon coconut oil, melted

8 ounces mixed leafy greens, such as bok choy, kale, or tatsoi, finely sliced

Put the tofu cubes in a large bowl with the mustard seeds, black onion seeds, salt, and five-spice powder and toss to coat.

Bring 1⅔ cups water to a boil in a small saucepan. Add the miso paste and stir to dissolve. Remove from the heat.

Heat the coconut oil in a skillet. Add the greens and sauté for 2 to 3 minutes, until tender. Layer the greens and tofu in serving bowls, pour the white miso broth over the top, and serve.

HARISSA CAULIFLOWER AND CORN

Cauliflower acts as a blank canvas that goes well with other flavors. It's the perfect ingredient for a soup that satisfies

Serves 2 / 239 calories

1 tablespoon extra-virgin olive oil

½ medium onion, finely chopped

1 teaspoon rose harissa

½ medium cauliflower (about 1 pound), cut into small florets

1¼ cups hot vegetable stock (page 75)

1 ear corn, steamed or boiled, kernels removed, or 1 cup frozen corn kernels

Sea salt and freshly ground pepper

Heat the olive oil in a Dutch oven and sauté the onion until soft and translucent, about 10 minutes. Add the rose harissa and stir it into the onion, then add the cauliflower and stir to combine.

After a couple of minutes, add the hot stock and simmer for 7 to 10 minutes, or until the cauliflower is tender but still has a little bite. Add the corn and heat through.

Transfer half the soup to a blender and blend until smooth, then taste and adjust the seasoning. Divide the blended soup between two bowls and top with the remaining unblended soup.

BUTTERNUT SQUASH AND HORSERADISH

The mustardy spice of the horseradish, often used as an herbal remedy for colds, pairs well with the sweetness of the butternut squash.

Serves 2 / 239 calories

2 tablespoons extra-virgin olive oil

1 pound butternut squash, peeled, seeded, and cut into small cubes

½ teaspoon grated fresh horseradish, or 1 teaspoon prepared horseradish

Zest of ½ lemon

1¼ cups hot chicken or vegetable stock (pages 70 and 75)

3 tablespoons almond milk

Small handful of fresh tarragon

1 tablespoon Cleanse Dukkah (page 66)

Heat the olive oil in a Dutch oven. Add the squash and sauté for about 5 minutes. Stir in the horseradish and lemon zest, then the hot stock. Bring to a boil, then reduce the heat to maintain a simmer. Cook until the squash can be easily pierced with a knife, 5 to 8 minutes.

Remove from the heat and set aside a couple of spoonfuls of squash cubes. Add the almond milk and tarragon to the soup. Blend in a food processor until smooth.

To serve, divide the soup between two bowls and spoon in the reserved squash. Sprinkle with the dukkah.

KITCHARI

This soup recipe for kitchari is based on the ancient medicine tradition of Ayurveda that will get rid of any bloating or water retention and have you feeling light on your toes in no time.

Serves 2 / 219 calories

3 to 4 ounces green mung beans

1 teaspoon ground turmeric

¼ teaspoon asafetida

2 tablespoons coconut oil, melted

1 teaspoon Cleanse Spice Mix (page 66)

Zest and juice of 1 lime

Sea salt and freshly ground black pepper

Plain Greek yogurt, for serving

Rinse the mung beans in several changes of water, then put them in a bowl with water to cover and soak overnight. Rinse and drain the beans again. Put them in a saucepan with 1 quart fresh water. Bring to a boil and add the turmeric and asafetida. Reduce the heat to maintain a simmer and cook gently for 45 minutes to 1 hour, until the beans are soft.

Heat half the coconut oil in a skillet and add the cleanse spices and lime zest. Toast until the spices become fragrant, then add to the soup along with the lime juice. Taste and adjust the seasoning, add the remaining coconut oil, and cover the skillet. Remove from the heat and let the soup stand for 10 minutes.

Divide between two bowls and serve each with a spoonful of yogurt.

LEMON CHICKEN AND MINT

Lemon juice is thought to be beneficial for digestion, which is why it's good to start the day with a cup of hot lemon water. The pectin found in lemon zest is a particularly good source of fiber that helps you to feel satisfied after a meal.

Serves 2 / 174 calories

3½ cups chicken stock (page 70)

2 boneless, skinless chicken thighs

Zest and juice of 1 lemon, zest cut into thin strips

Handful of fresh mint leaves, chopped

Bring the chicken stock to a boil in a large saucepan. Add the chicken thighs, lemon zest, and mint (reserve about 1 tablespoon of mint for serving), and reduce the heat to a simmer. Poach gently for 10 to 15 minutes, until the chicken is cooked through. Remove the chicken from the pan, let it cool a little, then slice it into thin strips.

Bring the broth back to a simmer. Add the chicken and lemon juice. Taste to see if more lemon juice is necessary.

To serve, stir in the reserved chopped mint and ladle the soup into bowls.

PEA AND PRESERVED LEMON

As part of the legume family (foods that come in a pod), green peas are a great source of antioxidants. Keep a bag of frozen peas on hand so you can make this soup in just five minutes whenever the mood strikes.

Serves 1 / 134 calories

½ cup chicken stock (page 70)

Pinch of red pepper flakes

1 cup frozen peas

4 ounces plain Greek yogurt, plus more for serving

1 teaspoon finely chopped preserved lemon

Handful of fresh dill, chopped

Combine the stock and red pepper flakes in a saucepan. Bring to a boil, then reduce the heat to maintain a simmer. Add the peas and simmer for 2 to 3 minutes, until cooked but still with a little bite.

Stir together the yogurt, preserved lemon, and dill in a bowl. To serve, either leave the peas whole or puree the soup directly in the pot with an immersion blender or transfer to a food processor and puree. Ladle into a bowl and serve with the yogurt mixture.

TOMATO AND LEMON SOUP WITH SALSA

Tomatoes are one of the best sources of heart- and bone-healthy lycopene. They are also a taste of summer.

Serves 2 / 133 calories

1 pound cherry tomatoes on the vine

1 tablespoon extra-virgin olive oil

1 tablespoon balsamic vinegar

1 teaspoon grated lemon zest

Sea salt

1½ teaspoons capers, rinsed, drained, and chopped

1 spring onion, thinly sliced

1 cup hot vegetable stock (page 70)

1 tablespoon tomato paste

Wheat-free seeded flatbreads, for serving (optional)

Preheat the oven to 450°F. Reserve a handful of the tomatoes. Arrange the remaining tomatoes on a baking sheet. Drizzle with the olive oil and vinegar, sprinkle with the lemon zest, and season with a little sea salt. Roast for 10 minutes, until the tomatoes are bursting. Turn off the oven and allow the tomatoes to continue to soften in the residual heat.

Meanwhile, make the salsa by chopping the remaining cherry tomatoes and mixing them with the capers and onion in a small bowl.

Remove the roasted cherry tomatoes from the vines and put them in a blender or a food processor with the hot stock and tomato paste and blend until smooth.

To serve, garnish the soup with the salsa or serve the salsa on the side with seeded flatbreads.

SAFFRON BROTH WITH SHRIMP

Saffron is mostly associated with risotto, but when you allow it to infuse stock, its flavor shines through. If you prefer, enjoy the saffron broth and vegetables without the shrimp.

Serves 2 / 133 calories

4 baby leeks

4 baby carrots

4 baby fennel

2 cups vegetable stock (page 70)

A few strands of saffron

Sea salt

6 ounces shrimp, cooked and peeled

Freshly ground black pepper

Lemon wedges, for serving

Trim the vegetables and put them in a wide saucepan. Add the stock, saffron, and a good pinch of sea salt. Bring to a boil, reduce the heat to maintain a simmer, and cook until the vegetables are al dente. Taste and adjust the seasoning.

To serve, ladle the saffron vegetable broth into bowls and add the shrimp. Divide the soup between two bowls and serve with the lemon wedges.

SICHUAN PEPPERCORNS AND CHICKEN

We have noticed that many Western trends in healthy food have their roots in ancient Eastern traditions, such as Ayurveda and Chinese medicine. Sichuan peppercorns are said to warm the body, reduce damp, and support digestion.

Serves 2 / 268 calories

2 cups seaweed stock (page 72)

6 scallions: 3 cut into 1-inch pieces, 3 finely sliced

1 (½-inch) piece fresh ginger, peeled and thinly sliced

2 star anise pods

½ teaspoon Sichuan peppercorns

1 tablespoon tamari (wheat-free soy sauce)

2 large boneless, skinless chicken thighs, or 1 cup shredded cooked chicken

1 tablespoon toasted sesame oil

8 ounces collard or turnip greens, rinsed, stemmed, and shredded

Bring the seaweed stock to a boil in a saucepan, then reduce the heat to maintain a simmer. Add the scallions, ginger, star anise, Sichuan peppercorns, and tamari. Simmer for 15 minutes to infuse the stock.

Add the chicken thighs (but not the cooked chicken, if using) and poach for about 10 minutes, or until cooked through. Remove the thighs from the stock. When cool enough to handle, use your fingers to shred the meat.

Heat the sesame oil in a skillet over medium heat. Add the collard greens and sauté for 5 minutes, tossing frequently.

Pass the stock through a sieve into a clean pot. Stir the chicken and greens into the stock. Taste and adjust the seasoning before ladling into individual bowls.

SMOKED EGGPLANT AND KEFIR

With its rich texture, eggplant makes a great vegetarian alternative to meat. By cooking the eggplant directly over a flame, you don't need to add any oil. Once the eggplant has been cooked on all sides, the charred skin is discarded.

Serves 2 / 135 calories

2 medium eggplants

4 ounces kefir

½ cup vegetable stock (page 75)

1 garlic clove

1 tablespoon plain Greek yogurt

Zest of ½ lime

Extra-virgin olive oil, for serving

Rye bread, for serving

Holding the eggplants carefully with long-handled tongs, char them directly over a gas flame on your stovetop or on a grill. Turn them as the skin chars on each side until the flesh is soft within. When they are completely charred and softened, place them in a bowl and cover with plastic wrap until cool, to make them easy to peel. Peel and seed the eggplants.

Bring the kefir, stock, and garlic to a boil in a saucepan. Add the eggplant flesh, reduce the heat to maintain a simmer, and cook for 10 minutes. Let cool slightly before adding the yogurt and lime zest and pureeing directly in the pot with an immersion blender (alternatively, transfer the soup to a blender or food processor and puree).

Serve drizzled with olive oil and with a slice of rye bread alongside.

HOT SMOKED MUSHROOM

Smoking the mushrooms is optional here. In her work as a chef, Nicole would happily smoke anything. At home, we use a large roasting tray that has a lid. If you'd rather, sauté the mushrooms all together, just adding a little more coconut oil.

Serves 2 / 100 calories

Earl Grey or green tea leaves

Uncooked rice

3 to 4 ounces button mushrooms

1 tablespoon coconut oil

3 or 4 brown mushrooms, sliced

1 garlic clove, crushed

3 tablespoons almond milk

½ cup hot vegetable or chicken stock (pages 75 and 70)

Lay a mixture of tea leaves (Earl Grey or green) and rice on the bottom of a baking pan, set a wire rack over the top, and put the button mushrooms on the rack. Cover the pan with a lid or aluminum foil. Set the pan on the stovetop over high heat and when it starts to smoke (check every minute or so by taking a look under the lid), reduce the heat to low. Smoke the button mushrooms for about 35 minutes.

Heat the coconut oil in a skillet. Add the brown mushrooms and sauté until soft, adding the garlic after a minute or two. Remove from the pan. Pour in the almond milk and stir, scraping up any browned bits on the bottom of the pan, then add the hot stock and simmer for a few minutes.

Add the smoked mushrooms to the pan. Blend directly in the pot with an immersion blender or transfer to a blender or food processor and blend to the desired consistency.

SPINACH AND SPICED ONION

Adding quinoa to vegetables before blending creates a creamy texture without the need for cream.

Serves 2 / 180 calories

1 tablespoon coconut oil

1 medium onion, sliced

¼ teaspoon ground cloves

½ cup quinoa

1⅔ cups hot vegetable stock (page 75)

6 ounces baby spinach

8 to 10 fresh basil leaves

Sea salt and freshly ground black pepper

2 tablespoons plain Greek yogurt, for serving (optional)

Heat the coconut oil in a Dutch oven. Add the onion and sauté for 10 minutes, until soft and just turning golden. Push the onions to the side of the pot with a wooden spoon. Stir in the cloves, and once they become fragrant, stir to combine with the onion and cook for 1 minute. Transfer half the onion to a plate.

Add the quinoa and the stock to the pot. Simmer for 15 minutes. Remove the pot from the heat, then add the spinach and basil. Blend the soup directly in the pot using an immersion blender or in a food processor until smooth. Taste and adjust the seasoning.

To serve, reheat the reserved onions in a skillet, ladle the soup into bowls, and top with the onions and yogurt, if desired.

SPRING CHICKEN

Leftover roast chicken with some crunchy spring cabbage and spicy mustard makes a perfect midweek meal.

Serves 2 / 302 calories

1 tablespoon peanut oil

½ cup finely shredded cabbage

1 cup shredded cooked chicken

1 tablespoon Umami Mustard (page 65) or grainy Dijon mustard

1 ⅔ cups hot chicken stock (page 70)

Sea salt and freshly ground black pepper

Heat the peanut oil in a skillet and when it begins to smoke, add the cabbage and stir-fry for 2 minutes. Add the chicken and mustard and stir for 30 seconds before adding the hot stock. Bring to a boil, then reduce the heat to maintain a simmer, and cook for a few minutes to let the flavors infuse. Taste and adjust the seasoning before serving.

TOFU SEAWEED MISO

If you like, stir in a handful of baby spinach, shredded kale, or bean sprouts during the last minute.

Serves 1 / 340 calories

1 cup cubed firm tofu

½ teaspoon ground turmeric

1 tablespoon toasted sesame oil

2 to 3 ounces wakame, rinsed

1 (1-ounce) miso soup mix packet

Toss the tofu in a bowl with the ground turmeric and sesame oil.

Bring a saucepan of water to a boil. Add the wakame, reduce the heat to maintain a simmer, and cook until the seaweed is al dente, 5 to 8 minutes.

Make the miso soup according to the packet instructions. Pour into a bowl, add the wakame and tofu, and serve.

SMOKED TOFU, TOMATO, AND BROCCOLI

Tofu adds a creaminess to the tomato soup base and makes a perfect backdrop to the deep green, crunchy broccoli.

Serves 2 / 111 calories

1 medium tomato, coarsely chopped

1 cup vegetable stock (page 75)

Sea salt and freshly ground black pepper

8 to 10 cherry tomatoes, chopped

¼ cup chopped sun-dried tomatoes

1.75 ounces smoked tofu

2 ounces broccoli florets

1 teaspoon hemp seeds

Place the medium tomato in a pan with the stock. Bring to a boil, then reduce the heat to maintain a simmer. Season with a little salt and pepper.

Add the cherry tomatoes and simmer for 15 minutes. Finely chop half the sun-dried tomatoes and add them to the pan. Remove from the heat and add the tofu. Blend directly in the pot using an immersion blender or transfer to a blender or a food processor until smooth. Pass the soup through a sieve.

Boil or steam the broccoli, drain, cool, and then chop into bite-size pieces. Place in a bowl and add the remainder of the sun-dried tomatoes, a drizzle of the tomato oil, and the hemp seeds. Mix to combine.

Warm the soup, divide it between two bowls, and top with the broccoli salad.

RESTORE

AUTUMN CHICKEN

Mushrooms are good sources of vitamins B and D. Studies suggest that they may be beneficial for our immune systems. Regardless, they are a wonderful autumnal addition to soups. Tarragon goes particularly well with mushrooms.

Serves 2 / 266 calories

1 tablespoon peanut oil

3 to 4 ounces wild mushrooms, such as chanterelle or oyster

1⅔ cups chicken stock (page 70)

1 cup shredded cooked chicken

Sea salt and freshly ground black pepper

Small handful of tarragon leaves, chopped

Heat the peanut oil in a skillet. Add the mushrooms and sauté until soft.

In a separate pan, heat the stock and add the chicken. Add the mushrooms to the stock and simmer for a couple of minutes. Taste and adjust the seasoning before serving with the chopped tarragon scattered on top.

BUCKWHEAT BROTH

Buckwheat is an ancient plant that produces grainlike seeds, which are an excellent gluten-free alternative to wheat. It contains protein and essential amino acids. Buckwheat is used in soba noodles, and the groats, or seeds, are delicious in soups and salads.

Serves 2 / 295 calories

2½ cups vegetable stock (page 75)

1 lemongrass stalk, smashed

3½ ounces buckwheat groats (kasha)

1 tablespoon coconut oil, melted

3 to 4 ounces kale leaves

1 (1-inch) piece fresh ginger, peeled and finely grated

Pinch of red pepper flakes

2 tablespoons tamari (wheat-free soy sauce)

Bring the stock to a boil in a saucepan, then reduce the heat to maintain a simmer. Add the lemongrass and the buckwheat and cook until the buckwheat is tender, about 15 minutes. Remove the pan from the heat and discard the lemongrass.

Heat the coconut oil in a skillet. Add the kale, ginger, and red pepper flakes and sauté until soft, then add a good splash of tamari.

To serve, divide the kale between two bowls and ladle the buckwheat broth over the top.

BUTTERNUT SQUASH AND SAGE

Any winter squash—butternut, acorn, Hubbard, kabocha—can be used in this warming soup.

Serves 2 / 309 calories

2 tablespoons extra-virgin olive oil

6 large fresh sage leaves

½ butternut squash, peeled, seeded, and chopped

1 onion, quartered

2 cups hot vegetable or chicken stock (pages 75 and 70)

Sea salt and freshly ground black pepper

Plain Greek yogurt, for serving

Preheat the oven to 400°F.

Heat the olive oil in a skillet. Add the sage leaves and cook until crispy, then remove the leaves and set aside to drain on a paper towel. Reserve the oil in the skillet.

Place the squash pieces and onion in a large bowl and add the sage-infused oil, tossing to combine thoroughly. Transfer the vegetables to a roasting pan. Roast for 45 minutes, until the squash is soft when pierced with a fork and slightly caramelized. Transfer the squash and stock to a blender and puree until smooth. Taste and adjust the seasoning.

Divide the soup between two bowls and top with some Greek yogurt and the crispy sage leaves.

CARDAMOM COCONUT BARLEY

This recipe is packed with spices known to improve digestion, lean protein, and slow-release grains. It will keep you energized.

Serves 2 / 413 calories

½ cup pearl barley

¼ cup coconut oil

2 tablespoons grated fresh ginger

3 garlic cloves, crushed

10 curry leaves

1 Thai chile, finely chopped

¼ teaspoon finely grated fresh turmeric or 1 teaspoon ground turmeric

1 teaspoon cumin seeds

1 teaspoon fennel seeds

1½ teaspoons black mustard seeds

2 cups coconut milk

6 cardamom pods

1 tablespoon peanut oil

4 ounces chopped turkey meat

Bunch of fresh cilantro, chopped, for serving

Bunch of scallions, chopped, for serving

Combine the barley and 1½ cups water in a saucepan. Bring to a boil, then reduce the heat to low, cover, and cook until tender, about 45 minutes. Let stand for a few minutes for the barley to absorb any remaining water.

Melt the coconut oil in a skillet. Add the ginger, garlic, curry leaves, and chile and sauté until fragrant. Add the turmeric, cumin, fennel, and black mustard seeds and sauté until the spices release their aromas and the mustard seeds just begin to pop. Remove from the heat and let the spices cool. Transfer the spices to a food processor and process to a paste.

Bring the coconut milk to a boil in a saucepan. Crush the cardamom pods with the back of a spoon, then add them to the coconut milk. Simmer for 10 minutes to infuse. Strain through a sieve to remove the pods, then discard them.

Heat the peanut oil in a saucepan. Add the turkey and cook, stirring occasionally, until the meat loses its raw color. Stir in a tablespoon of the spice paste.

Add the infused coconut milk and the
cooked barley and simmer for 5 minutes.
Ladle into bowls and sprinkle on plenty of
cilantro and scallions. Any leftover spice
paste can be refrigerated in an airtight
container for up to 2 weeks.

CARROT, CUMIN, AND MISO SOUP WITH GRAIN SALAD

To help calm the mind, you need to calm and gently nourish the digestive system, as the two are intrinsically linked. The digestive system likes naturally sweet foods, such as carrots and squash, and also gentle aromatic herbs and spices such as cinnamon, cumin, and basil.

Serves 2 / 179 calories

For the Soup

1 tablespoon coconut oil, melted

½ onion, sliced

½ teaspoon cumin seeds

1 pound carrots, coarsely chopped

½ teaspoon white miso paste

For the Salad

¼ cup buckwheat groats (kasha)

2 tablespoons dried cranberries, soaked in ½ cup warm water for 10 minutes, then drained

¼ onion, finely chopped

¼ celery stalk, finely chopped

¼ carrot, finely chopped

To make the soup, heat the coconut oil in a large pan. Add the onion and cook for 10 minutes, until soft. Push the onion to one side to create space in the pan and add the cumin seeds. When the seeds start to release their aroma, stir in the carrots. Stir in the miso paste. Add 1⅔ cups of boiling water. Bring everything to a boil, then reduce the heat to maintain a simmer and cook for 10 minutes, or until the carrots can be easily pierced with a knife. Blend the soup directly in the pan with an immersion blender or transfer to a blender or food processor and puree until smooth.

To make the salad, put the grains in a pan, add water to cover, and bring to a boil. Reduce the heat to maintain a simmer and cook until the grains are tender (check the package for cooking times). Drain the grains and transfer them to a large bowl. Add the cranberries, onion, celery, and carrot and stir to combine.

Serve the soup topped with some of the grain salad.

CARROT, GINGER, AND TANGERINE

This soup packs a vitamin C punch, while the carrot and ginger are warming and good for digestion.

Serves 2 / 146 calories

1 tablespoon extra-virgin olive oil

½ onion, sliced

1 celery stalk, sliced

4 carrots, scrubbed if organic, peeled if not, and chopped

½ teaspoon grated fresh ginger

Zest and juice of 1 tangerine

1¾ cups hot vegetable stock (page 75)

Cleanse Dukkah (page 66), for serving

Heat the olive oil in a Dutch oven. Add the onion and celery and gently sauté until soft and translucent. Add the carrots, ginger, and tangerine zest, stirring them to combine.

Cook for a couple of minutes before adding the hot stock. Bring to a boil, then reduce the heat to maintain a simmer and cook for about 10 minutes, or until the carrots are soft enough to be easily pierced with a knife.

Let cool a little before blending the soup directly in the pot with an immersion blender until smooth. Add half the tangerine juice, stir to combine, and check to see if you need more.

To serve, ladle into bowls and top with a sprinkle of dukkah.

CELERY ROOT AND UMAMI MUSTARD

Celery root (or celeriac) is often underrated because it's not the most attractive vegetable. We've taken the flavors of classic celeriac rémoulade and turned them into this soup.

Serves 2 / 199 calories

2 tablespoons extra-virgin olive oil

1 small celery root, peeled and cut into ½-inch cubes

1 teaspoon Umami Mustard (page 65)

1 cup hot vegetable stock (page 75)

Heat the olive oil in a large skillet. Add the celery root and sauté until golden brown. Add the mustard and stir to combine, then add the hot stock. Bring to a boil, then reduce the heat to maintain a simmer and cook until the celery root is cooked through and easily pierced with a knife, about 10 minutes.

Let cool a little before processing to a smooth consistency in a blender or food processor. Taste to check that you have added enough mustard to suit your taste.

CHICKEN CONGEE

White rice is more processed than brown, so it does convert to sugar more quickly in the body. We have included it, however, as an option in this Restore recipe since white rice is easy on the digestive system, and will help it build up strength if digestion is strained. Use brown rice, if you prefer; just increase the cooking time. Make this when you're struggling with stress or exhaustion and need to recuperate.

Serves 2 / 388 calories

1 cup white or brown rice

3 cups chicken stock (page 70)

1 (2-inch) piece fresh ginger, peeled and sliced

1 cup shredded cooked chicken

2 scallions, thinly sliced on an angle

2 tablespoons tamari (wheat-free soy sauce)

1 tablespoon toasted sesame oil

2 teaspoons furikake or a mixture of black and white sesame seeds

Handful of fresh cilantro leaves, for serving

Combine the rice, stock, ginger, and 1 quart water in a saucepan and bring to a boil. Cover and reduce the heat to maintain a simmer and cook for about an hour, until the rice has broken down (brown rice will take longer).

To serve, ladle the congee into bowls and top with the chicken and scallions. Sprinkle on some tamari and toasted sesame oil, followed by furikake and cilantro leaves.

CINNAMON PUMPKIN

With both cinnamon and sweet winter squash, this is a warming soup for the digestion. It is perfect for the colder months.

Serves 2 / 116 calories

1 sweet pumpkin, butternut squash, or other winter squash (about 14 ounces), peeled, seeded, and cut into cubes

1 tablespoon peanut oil

1 teaspoon ground cinnamon

8 to 10 ounces cherry tomatoes

1 tablespoon balsamic vinegar

1 cup hot vegetable stock (page 75)

Preheat the oven to 425°F.

In a large bowl, toss the pumpkin cubes with the peanut oil and cinnamon. Place on a baking sheet and roast for 30 minutes, or until slightly brown and cooked through when pierced with a fork. After 15 minutes, turn the pumpkin cubes. When cooked, add the cherry tomatoes to the baking sheet and splash with the balsamic vinegar.

Return the pan to the oven and turn it off; the residual heat will be enough to lightly roast the tomatoes. Remove the pan from the oven after 10 minutes.

Set aside half the tomatoes. Put the remaining tomatoes, the pumpkin, and the stock in a blender and puree. Pour the soup into bowls and top with the reserved tomatoes.

COD LAKSA

The Laksa Paste lifts the flavors of lemongrass and lime leaves in this soup.

Serves 1 / 258 calories

4 ounces cod fillet

2 teaspoons Laksa Paste (page 63)

1 teaspoon coconut oil

1 cup vegetable stock (page 75)

1 bok choy, coarsely chopped

Sea salt and freshly ground black pepper

Brush the cod fillet with 1 teaspoon of the Laksa Paste on the flesh side. Melt the coconut oil in a skillet. Add the fish, skin side down, and cook until the cod starts to sweat. Turn the fish over, then after a few seconds turn off the heat and let the fish sit.

Bring the stock to a boil in a saucepan. Stir in the remaining 1 teaspoon Laksa Paste to dissolve. Taste and add more paste, if you like. Add the bok choy to the pan and simmer for a minute before removing from the heat.

To serve, flake the cod into a bowl and ladle over the broth and vegetables.

CUMIN-ROASTED SWEET POTATO WITH ONION AND POMEGRANATE MOLASSES

We've used cumin here, but feel free to substitute ground cinnamon, cardamom, or ginger instead. Pomegranate molasses adds a little sweetness.

Serves 2 / 295 calories

2 large sweet potatoes, peeled and coarsely chopped

1 medium onion, sliced

1 teaspoon cumin seeds

1 teaspoon ground turmeric

2 tablespoons extra-virgin olive oil

1 tablespoon pomegranate molasses

2 cups hot vegetable stock (page 75)

Preheat the oven to 400°F.

Mix all the ingredients except the stock in a large bowl so the vegetables are evenly coated with the spices, olive oil, and molasses.

Transfer to a baking sheet and roast the vegetables for 15 to 20 minutes, turning halfway through, until the sweet potatoes are soft and caramelized at the edges. Let cool a little before blending the vegetables with the stock to the desired consistency.

GINGER CARROT WITH SPICED COCONUT YOGURT

The warmth of ginger is balanced by the cooling coconut yogurt. It's a simple, yet always winning, combination.

Serves 2 / 384 calories

For the Soup

1 tablespoon peanut oil

½ onion, chopped (optional)

1 teaspoon grated fresh ginger

1 pound carrots, scrubbed if organic, peeled if not, and coarsely chopped

1¾ cups hot vegetable stock (page 75)

Sea salt and freshly ground black pepper

For the Yogurt

1 tablespoon grated fresh or dried coconut

3 tablespoons plain Greek yogurt

1 tablespoon peanut oil

6 curry leaves

2 teaspoons black mustard seeds

To make the soup, heat the peanut oil in a saucepan. Add the onion (if using) and sauté for about 10 minutes until soft. Add the ginger and stir for a minute before adding the carrots. Continue to cook, stirring, for a couple of minutes, then add the stock, bring to a boil, and reduce the heat to maintain a simmer. Cook for 10 to 15 minutes, or until the carrots can be easily pierced with a knife. Process the soup in a blender or food processor until smooth. Taste and adjust the seasoning.

To make the coconut yogurt, mix the coconut with the yogurt in a small bowl. Heat the oil in a skillet and add the curry leaves, allowing them to infuse for a minute before adding the mustard seeds. When the seeds begin to pop, remove the pan from the heat, let cool a little, and then pour over the coconut yogurt.

To serve the soup, ladle into bowls and spoon over the spiced coconut yogurt.

JERUSALEM ARTICHOKE AND FENNEL

Jerusalem artichokes are nature's prebiotics and help create a fertile environment for your gut flora to flourish.

Serves 2 / 314 calories

10 ounces Jerusalem artichokes

1 teaspoon fresh lemon juice

2 tablespoons extra-virgin olive oil, plus more for serving

½ onion, chopped

1 celery stalk, chopped

½ fennel bulb, chopped

1½ cups hot chicken or vegetable stock (pages 70 and 75)

Sea salt

Cleanse Dukkah (page 66), for serving

Scrub the artichokes and soak them for a couple of hours in cold water with the lemon juice. Drain and coarsely chop them.

Heat the olive oil in a Dutch oven. Add the onion, celery, and fennel and sauté for 10 to 15 minutes, until soft. Add the artichokes and continue to cook for a few minutes more, then add the hot stock. Bring to a boil, then reduce the heat to maintain a simmer and cook for 10 to 15 minutes, or until the artichokes are soft. Puree in a blender or food processor until smooth, then taste and adjust the seasoning.

To serve, ladle into bowls, sprinkle with dukkah, and drizzle with olive oil.

LENTILS, SEASONAL GREENS, AND GINGER-CARROT COLESLAW

Green lentils from Puy, France, are considered by many to be the best. In this recipe, lentils are cooked like risotto. They are a great vegetarian source of protein. If you can't find Puy lentils, use brown ones.

Serves 2 / 343 calories

1 tablespoon extra-virgin olive oil

½ onion, finely chopped

⅔ cup Le Puy or brown lentils

1¾ cups hot vegetable stock (page 75)

1 large or 2 small carrots, scrubbed if organic, peeled if not, and grated

½ teaspoon grated fresh ginger

4 ounces kale, chard, or spinach, steamed, drained, and chopped

2 large egg yolks

Heat the olive oil in a skillet. Add the onion and sauté until soft, 8 to 10 minutes. Add the lentils and stir for a minute before adding the hot stock. Simmer for about 30 minutes, until the lentils are cooked, but still have a little bite.

Stir the carrot and ginger together.

To serve, divide the lentils and broth between two bowls and top with the carrot and greens. Stir one egg yolk into each bowl of hot soup.

MAGIC SOUP

This soup includes a mix of spices to stoke your digestive fires back to strength.

Serves 2 / 343 calories

1 heaping cup yellow split peas, rinsed

¼ teaspoon cayenne pepper

½ teaspoon ground turmeric

1 tablespoon coconut oil

1 onion, sliced

½ teaspoon ground cinnamon

½ teaspoon ground ginger

½ teaspoon garam masala

6 to 8 ounces baby spinach

2 tablespoons toasted mixed seeds (pumpkin, sesame, hemp, flax), for serving

Put the split peas in a saucepan with 1 quart water, the cayenne pepper, and the turmeric and bring to a boil. Reduce the heat to maintain a simmer and cook gently for about 1 hour, or until the split peas are soft and broken up. Transfer half the split peas to a blender or food processor and process until smooth, then return them to the pan and stir them into the reserved split peas.

Heat the coconut oil in a large skillet. Add the onion and cook gently for about 10 minutes, until soft. Add the spices and cook until aromatic. Add the spinach to the pan and stir through to wilt.

Warm the split pea soup, divide it between two serving bowls, and top with the spiced spinach and onions. Sprinkle with the mixed seeds.

ROASTED BUCKWHEAT WITH ACHARI SPICES AND EXOTIC MUSHROOMS

Mushrooms such as shiitake, enoki, cremini, and oyster contain properties that stimulate the immune system. To toast the buckwheat groats, put them in a skillet over medium heat and cook, stirring regularly, until fragrant.

Serves 2 / 305 calories

1 tablespoon peanut oil

1 small onion, finely chopped

½ teaspoon cumin seeds

½ teaspoon fennel seeds

½ teaspoon mustard seeds

½ teaspoon ground turmeric

⅔ cup buckwheat groats (kasha), toasted

1¾ cups hot vegetable stock (page 75)

1 tablespoon coconut oil

3 to 4 ounces mushrooms, such as shiitake, enoki, and oyster

Heat the peanut oil in a saucepan. Add the onion and sauté until soft. Add the cumin, fennel, mustard seeds, and turmeric. Stir until the spices become fragrant. Stir in the buckwheat groats. Add enough hot stock to cover the buckwheat. Cook for about 20 minutes, or until tender.

Meanwhile, heat the coconut oil in a skillet. Add the mushrooms and sauté until light golden.

To serve, ladle the buckwheat broth into bowls and top with the mushrooms.

SPROUTED SOUP

A soup made with just beans and spices gets an added nutritional boost from live sprouts sprinkled on top.

Serves 2 / 245 calories

½ **cup dried adzuki beans, soaked for 48 hours (change the water 3 times daily) and rinsed**

2 cups hot vegetable stock (page 75)

1 teaspoon ground turmeric

2 tablespoons light sesame oil or extra-virgin olive oil

1 teaspoon Cleanse Spice Mix (page 66)

2 tablespoons radish or alfalfa sprouts, for serving

Kefir or plain Greek yogurt, for serving

Combine the beans, hot stock, and turmeric in a saucepan. Bring to a boil, then reduce the heat to maintain a simmer and cook for about 1 hour, until the beans are tender.

Meanwhile, heat the sesame oil in a skillet. Add the spice mix and cook, stirring frequently, until the spices become fragrant. Remove the skillet from the heat and let cool for a bit, then add the spice mix to the soup and give it a good stir.

Serve the soup topped with a handful of sprouted seeds and a spoonful of kefir or plain Greek yogurt.

WHITE KIMCHI

Our take on cabbage soup is more interesting and flavorful when the probiotic powers of fermented kimchi and miso broth are added. Add some cooked soba noodles if it's not quite satisfying enough.

Serves 1 / 118 calories

1 cup white miso stock

2 heaping tablespoons Kimchi (page 67)

½ cup cubed silken tofu

1 scallion, thinly sliced, for serving

1 teaspoon white sesame seeds, for serving

Heat the miso stock in a saucepan. In a bowl, arrange the kimchi and the tofu, then pour the hot stock over the top. Sprinkle with the scallion and sesame seeds before serving.

RENEW

BARLEY BONE BROTH

This soup is warming and comforting. For one cup cooked barley, use one-third cup uncooked.

Serves 2 / 284 calories

1 tablespoon peanut oil

1 leek, thinly sliced

2 carrots, chopped

1 cup cooked barley

1⅔ cups hot bone broth (page 74)

Freshly ground black pepper

Heat the peanut oil in a saucepan. Add the leek and sauté until soft. Add the carrots and cook for a few minutes. Add the cooked barley and stir well. Stir in the hot broth and bring to a boil. Reduce the heat to maintain a simmer and cook until the carrot is tender but still has a little bite.

Season with plenty of pepper and serve.

BEETS AND CARAWAY

Caraway seeds may be beneficial to digestion and add a lovely flavor to the intensity of the beets.

Serves 2 / 136 calories

4 large or 6 small beets

2 tablespoons apple cider vinegar

1 teaspoon caraway seeds

1¾ cups hot vegetable stock (page 75)

2 tablespoons chopped fresh dill

Sea salt and freshly ground black pepper

Plain Greek yogurt, for serving

Preheat the oven to 400°F.

Wash the beets and cut off all but 1 to 2 inches of the tops. Place in a roasting pan and add enough water to come about half-way up the sides. Add the vinegar. Sprinkle on the caraway seeds, cover the pan with aluminum foil, and bake until soft, about 45 minutes.

Remove from the oven and take off the foil. Remove the beets from the cooking liquid and allow to cool, then rub off the skins with paper towels. Coarsely chop the beets, then blend with the stock and chopped dill until the desired consistency. Taste and adjust seasoning.

Serve warm or cold, with a dollop of yogurt.

CAULIFLOWER, GARLIC, AND WALNUT CRUMB

As part of the cruciferous family, cauliflower is supportive of the body's own detoxification system and contains both anti-oxidant and anti-inflammatory properties. Garlic is naturally anti-inflammatory, too, while in Chinese medicine, walnuts are said to support our "essence."

Serves 2 / 256 calories

1¼ cups almond milk

3 garlic cloves

½ medium cauliflower (about 1 pound), cut into florets

Sea salt and freshly ground black pepper

Drizzle of rosemary-infused oil (page 69), for serving

2 tablespoons chopped walnuts, for serving

Scald the almond milk in a saucepan. Add the garlic and simmer for 10 minutes. Remove the garlic and add the cauliflower. Simmer for 7 to 10 minutes, or until tender when pierced with a knife. Allow the soup to cool a little before blending in a blender or food processor until smooth. Taste and adjust the seasoning.

To serve, ladle the soup into bowls, drizzle with a swirl of rosemary oil, and sprinkle with the chopped walnuts.

CHICKEN AND NETTLE TOPS

Nettle soup is traditionally made in the spring as a fresh change from eating lots of preserved foods all winter. We might have access to fresh foods all year round now, but spring still feels like the perfect time to lighten things up and have a good cleanse, so keep this recipe on hand for when fresh young nettles appear at farmers' markets.

Serves 1 / 274 calories

½ cup chicken stock (page 70)

½ cup shredded cooked chicken

2 ounces nettle tops or baby spinach

2 tablespoons tamari (wheat-free soy sauce)

Bring the chicken stock to a boil in a pan. Reduce the heat to a simmer and add the chicken. After a couple of minutes add the nettle tops and simmer until wilted, just a minute or so.

Add the tamari, taste, and adjust the seasoning. Serve immediately.

FENNEL-CRUSTED SALMON WITH GINGER CABBAGE

Seeds such as fennel, cumin, or coriander and citrus zests and peels are the perfect way to add extra layers of taste, texture, and bonus nutrition to our cooking.

Serves 2 / 311 calories

1 teaspoon fennel seeds

Zest of 1 lime

1 teaspoon coconut oil

2 (6-ounce) salmon fillets, skin on

1 teaspoon Dijon mustard or Umami Mustard (page 65)

1¼ cups vegetable stock (page 75)

1 (1-inch) piece fresh ginger, peeled and thickly sliced

1 small napa cabbage, thickly sliced

Preheat the oven to 300°F.

Scatter the fennel seeds and lime zest on a baking sheet and toast in the oven for 10 minutes. Transfer to a mortar and pestle and crush the seeds. Raise the oven temperature to 425°F.

Heat the coconut oil in a skillet over medium heat. Add the salmon fillets, skin side down, and fry for about 3 minutes, until the skin is crisp. Remove the skillet from the heat. Brush some mustard on each fillet, then sprinkle on the fennel-lime mixture. Bake the fish for 5 minutes or longer, until it reaches the desired doneness.

Put the vegetable stock and ginger slices into a large saucepan along with the napa cabbage. Bring to a boil, then reduce the heat to maintain a simmer and cook for about 10 minutes, until the cabbage is cooked through but still has a nice bite to it.

To serve, place the cabbage in bowls and ladle over the broth. Flake the salmon and divide it between the bowls.

HARISSA BROTH WITH EGGPLANT AND QUINOA

This is a deeply flavored and nourishing soup.

Serves 2 / 194 calories

1 eggplant, sliced into 1½-inch-thick rounds

1½ tablespoons extra-virgin olive oil

Sea salt

1 cup vegetable stock (page 75)

1 teaspoon rose harissa

½ cup black or white quinoa

Saffron Yogurt (page 68), for serving

Preheat the oven to 475°F.

Place the eggplant rounds in a bowl and drizzle over the olive oil, combining thoroughly so that all the eggplant rounds are covered. Season with salt. Spread out the eggplant over a roasting pan and roast in the oven for 10 to 15 minutes, until golden, turning halfway through.

Meanwhile, bring the stock to a boil in a saucepan. Add the harissa and quinoa. Reduce the heat to maintain a simmer and cook for 8 minutes. Turn off the heat and allow to rest so the quinoa puffs.

Set aside 4 slices of eggplant, then quarter the remaining slices, adding the quarters to the quinoa and harissa broth. Stir in and let sit.

To serve, heat the soup and divide between two bowls. Set the eggplant rounds on top and dollop yogurt over the soup using a slotted spoon.

GREEN PHO

There are endless regional variations of pho, the national soup of Vietnam. Pho is most frequently eaten at breakfast, but feel free to enjoy it at any meal. Do add either some cubed tofu or brown rice noodles to the soup. Put the basics together the night before.

Serves 1 / 77 calories

1 teaspoon grated fresh ginger

½ Thai chile, seeded and finely sliced

2 scallions, finely sliced

3 to 4 ounces tatsoi baby bok choy, or other Asian greens, chopped

A few kaffir lime, fresh Thai basil leaves or cilantro leaves

Handful of bean sprouts

1 lime wedge

1 cup hot vegetable stock (page 75)

The night before you want to eat this soup, put all the ingredients except the lime and stock into a jar and mix well to combine.

To serve, pour the hot vegetable stock into the jar, squeeze over the lime, and stir to combine.

MUSSELS AND LEEK

Often shellfish will be left out of a cleanse because they may be high in heavy metals, picked up from the ocean floor. On the other hand, they are a rich source of many energizing vitamins and minerals. We go for a varied diet and so are happy to include shellfish on occasion. Treat yourself to a piece of sourdough to mop up the broth.

Serves 2 / 372 calories

2 pounds mussels, cleaned and debearded

1 tablespoon coconut oil

½ onion, finely chopped

½ celery stalk, finely chopped

1 leek, finely chopped

3 tablespoons sake (optional)

1 cup vegetable stock (page 75)

Check through the mussels, discarding any open ones that don't close when tapped firmly on the work surface.

Heat the oil in a heavy-bottomed saucepan. Add the onion and celery and cook gently for 5 minutes, then add the leek and cook for 10 minutes more. Add the sake (if using) and stock, then add the mussels. Give everything a good stir, cover with a lid, and then remove from the heat with the lid still on so the mussels cook in the residual heat. The mussels will open once cooked.

To serve, divide the mussels and leek broth between two bowls. Remove and discard any mussels that haven't opened.

RAW SOUP

This is perfect for a warm, sunny day.

Serves 2 / 194 calories

1 medium Hass avocado, pitted, peeled, and chopped

½ medium cucumber, coarsely chopped

Handful of baby spinach or kale leaves

Zest and juice of ½ lime, plus more juice to taste

⅓ cup plain Greek yogurt or kefir

3 ice cubes

Sea salt and freshly ground black pepper

2 scallions, finely chopped

1 tablespoon finely chopped fresh cilantro

Combine the avocado, cucumber, spinach, lime zest, lime juice, yogurt, and ice cubes in a food processor or blender. Puree until smooth. Add a little cold water if the soup seems too thick. Taste and adjust the seasoning, adding more lime, if needed. Transfer to the refrigerator to chill before serving.

Combine the chopped scallions and cilantro to make a salsa. Serve the chilled soup with a dollop of salsa on top.

RADISH, CRAB, AND TURMERIC CONGEE

Congee is rice that is slow-cooked in larger quantities of water than we are often used to. The rice is cooked until it breaks down and turns the liquid thick and creamy. The congee has a mild, sweet flavor and is incredibly easy on the digestion, which makes it nourishing.

Serves 2 / 316 calories

1 cup short-grain white rice, rinsed

4 cups chicken or vegetable stock (pages 75 and 70)

¼ teaspoon grated fresh turmeric, or 1 teaspoon ground turmeric

1 tablespoon toasted sesame oil

3½ to 4 ounces lump crabmeat, picked over

Small bunch breakfast radishes, thinly sliced

3 scallions, thinly sliced

1 (1-inch) piece fresh ginger, peeled and sliced into small matchstick pieces

2 teaspoons furikake or a mixture of black and white sesame seeds

Put the rice, stock, turmeric, and 3 cups water in a saucepan. Bring to a boil. Reduce the heat to maintain a simmer and cook for 30 to 90 minutes, depending on the consistency you prefer. Stir occasionally to prevent the rice from sticking to the bottom of the pan. The longer you can wait, the better!

Serve the congee in deep bowls and drizzle a little sesame oil over the top. Sprinkle with the crabmeat, radish slices, scallions, ginger, and furikake.

RED LENTIL AND TAMARIND

We love to come across different ways to make dal, and this combination of red lentils with tamarind is a new favorite.

Serves 2 / 204 calories

½ cup red lentils, rinsed

2 cups vegetable stock (page 75)

1 teaspoon ground turmeric

1 teaspoon garam masala

1 tablespoon tamarind paste

1 (1-inch) piece fresh ginger, peeled and grated

1 tablespoon tomato paste

½ cup cooked brown rice

2 tablespoons plain Greek yogurt or kefir

Fresh cilantro leaves, for serving

Combine the lentils, stock, turmeric, garam masala, tamarind paste, and ginger in a saucepan. Bring to a boil, then reduce the heat to maintain a simmer and cook until the lentils are soft, about 20 minutes, adding the tomato paste about halfway through.

Stir in the brown rice to heat through, then serve immediately with a spoonful of yogurt and some fresh cilantro leaves scattered over the top.

ROAST CHICKPEA

Chickpeas and paprika were made to go together. Apparently, chickpeas may even help to trigger feelings of satiety, useful when we are retraining our appetite after the holidays.

Serves 2 / 188 calories

⅓ cup chickpeas, soaked for 24 hours, drained, and rinsed

1 bay leaf

1 garlic clove, smashed

1 teaspoon Turkish or Aleppo pepper

1 teaspoon smoked paprika

1 teaspoon ground allspice

1 tablespoon tomato paste

1 tablespoon honey

1 red chile, seeded and sliced

Dash of apple cider vinegar

1 cup hot vegetable stock (page 75)

Bunch of fresh cilantro, chopped, for serving

Plain Greek yogurt or kefir, for serving

Put the chickpeas, bay leaf, and garlic in a saucepan and add water to cover. Bring to a boil, then reduce the heat to maintain a simmer and cook for 1 hour.

Preheat the oven to 425°F. Remove the bay leaf, drain the chickpeas, and combine them in a bowl along with all the dried spices, the tomato paste, honey, and chile and mix well. Arrange the chickpeas in a single layer on a rimmed baking sheet, add the vinegar, and roast for 10 to 15 minutes.

Transfer all or half the chickpeas (if you like a chunkier texture) and the hot stock to a blender or food processor and puree to the desired consistency.

Pour the soup into bowls. Garnish with the remaining chickpeas, if you only pureed half, chopped cilantro, and a spoonful of yogurt.

SESAME CHICKEN

In Chinese medicine it is said we deplete our "essence" by consuming too many stimulants and not enough minerals. We can help redress the balance through good rest, relaxation, and a nourishing diet that includes nutrient-dense foods such as chicken, seaweed, nettles, and sesame seeds. Furikake is a seasoning mixture of sesame seeds, chopped seaweed, and salt. If you can't find it, mix together some black and white sesame seeds.

Serves 2 / 362 calories

3 ounces soba or brown rice noodles

1 tablespoon peanut oil

1 (2-inch) piece ginger, peeled and finely sliced into matchsticks

4 large or 6 small fresh or dried shiitake mushrooms, soaked, if dried, and drained

2 boneless, skinless chicken thighs, cut into bite-size pieces

1 tablespoon brown rice vinegar

1¾ cups chicken stock (page 70)

2 teaspoons toasted sesame oil

1 teaspoon fish sauce

1 tablespoon tamari (wheat-free soy sauce)

2 scallions, thinly sliced on an angle

2 teaspoons furikake or a mixture of black and white sesame seeds

Bring a pan of water to a boil. Add the noodles and cook for 3 to 5 minutes or according to the package instructions. Drain the noodles, then rinse under cold water and drain again.

Heat the peanut oil in a wok over high heat. When the oil starts to smoke, add the ginger and mushrooms and stir-fry for a few seconds. Add the chicken and stir-fry until the chicken has browned a little, then add the vinegar to deglaze the wok. Add the stock, sesame oil, fish sauce, and tamari. Bring to a boil, then reduce the heat to maintain a simmer and cook for 10 minutes.

To serve, add the cooked noodles to the soup and ladle the soup into deep bowls. Sprinkle with the scallions and furikake.

Hot Cucumber with Barley
(page 94)

Salmon Poached in Lemongrass Tea *(page 97)*

Five-spice Tofu
(page 104)

Kitchari *(page 107)*

**Tomato and Lemon Soup
with Salsa** *(page 110)*

Carrot, Cumin, and Miso Soup
with Grain Salad
(page 124)

Magic Soup (page 134)

Raw Soup *(page 146)*

SOPA DI QUINOA

As a seed, rather than a grain, quinoa contains a large amount of protein. We love the black and red varieties, which are more readily available now, but use any variety.

Serves 2 / 381 calories

2 tablespoons pistachios, toasted

Good handful of fresh basil leaves

1 tablespoon Umami Mustard (page 65)

¼ cup extra-virgin olive oil

½ cup quinoa

1¼ cups vegetable stock (page 75)

4 to 5 ounces green beans, chopped

Sea salt

2 ounces pea shoots, for serving (optional)

Put the pistachios, basil, and mustard in a food processor and pulse three or four times. With the motor running, slowly pour in the olive oil and process to form a smooth pesto.

Combine the quinoa and stock in a saucepan. Bring to a boil, then reduce the heat to maintain a simmer and cook until the quinoa is al dente, 12 to 15 minutes.

Steam or boil the green beans until al dente and add to the quinoa broth. Taste and adjust the seasoning.

To serve, ladle the broth into bowls and add a spoonful of the pistachio pesto, then sprinkle with the pea shoots, if desired.

SQUASH AND ALMOND BUTTER

Not only do almonds contain heart-healthy monounsaturated fats, but they have been shown to help decrease blood sugar imbalances.

Serves 2 / 376 calories

1 tablespoon peanut oil

1 small onion, sliced

½ butternut squash, peeled and cut into cubes

1 carrot, scrubbed if organic, peeled if not, and chopped into cubes

2 cups hot vegetable or chicken stock (pages 75 and 70)

2 tablespoons crunchy almond butter

1 teaspoon chopped almonds, for serving

Plain Greek yogurt or kefir, for serving (optional)

Heat the peanut oil in a saucepan. Add the onion and sauté until soft and translucent, about 10 minutes. Add the squash and carrot and sauté for a few minutes, stirring occasionally.

Add the hot stock and the almond butter, bring to a boil, then reduce the heat to maintain a simmer and cook gently for 15 to 20 minutes, or until the vegetables are tender. Let cool a little, then transfer to a blender and puree to make a smooth soup.

Pour the soup into bowls and sprinkle the chopped almonds on top. Add a swirl of yogurt, if you like.

WATERCRESS, FLAX, AND TOFU

We challenged ourselves to make a creamy watercress soup without potatoes or cream. The secret is tofu.

Serves 2 / 248 calories

1¾ cups chicken or vegetable stock (pages 70 and 75)

3 ounces watercress

3 ounces spinach

2 tablespoons flaxseed meal

½ cup firm cubed tofu

Sea salt and freshly ground black pepper

Plain Greek yogurt, for serving

2 teaspoons toasted hemp seeds, for serving

1 tablespoon extra-virgin olive oil

Bring the stock to a boil in a saucepan. Add the watercress and spinach and stir just until limp. Remove the pan from the heat. After a couple of minutes, add the flaxseed meal and tofu cubes. Pour the soup into a blender or food processor and puree. Taste and adjust the seasoning.

Pour into bowls and serve topped with yogurt and the toasted hemp seeds. Drizzle with the olive oil.

WILD RICE, EDAMAME, AND RAINBOW CHARD

This soup is packed with nutrients from the dark leafy greens.

Serves 2 / 165 calories

¼ cup wild rice, rinsed

⅓ cup shelled edamame

2 ounces sea beans

1¼ cups seaweed broth
(page 72)

3½ ounces rainbow chard,
stems cut into 1-inch
pieces and leaves
shredded

Cleanse Dukkah (page
66), for serving

Put the rice in a saucepan, add water to cover, and bring to a boil. Reduce the heat to low, cover, and simmer until the rice is cooked, 35 to 40 minutes. Drain the rice.

In another saucepan of simmering water, blanch the edamame and sea beans for a couple of minutes. Drain.

Bring the seaweed broth to a boil in another saucepan. Stir in the drained rice and vegetables. Remove from the heat.

Divide the soup between two bowls. Sprinkle with some dukkah and serve.

WINTER CHICKEN

Rainbow chard is a variety of Swiss chard with a range of colorful stems—red, orange, and yellow. Like other dark leafy greens, it happily grows during the colder months in many climates.

Serves 2 / 336 calories

1 tablespoon peanut oil

1 leek, finely sliced

4 ounces rainbow chard, stems cut into 1-inch pieces and leaves shredded

1 cup shredded cooked chicken

1¾ cups hot chicken stock (page 70)

Sea salt and freshly ground black pepper

2 tablespoons plain Greek yogurt, for serving

1 tablespoon chopped hazelnuts, toasted, for serving

Heat the peanut oil in a Dutch oven. Add the leek and sauté until soft. Add the chard and cook for a couple of minutes, then add the chicken, followed by the hot stock. Bring to a boil, then reduce the heat to maintain a simmer and cook until the chard is cooked through, a few minutes. Taste and adjust the seasoning.

Ladle the soup into bowls and top each with a spoonful of the yogurt and the toasted hazelnuts.

Soup Jars

What a great way to take soup to work: just add hot water to the ingredients, stir it up, and enjoy! The idea behind the soup jar concept is to have the noodles or grain at the bottom of a sealable container, followed by layers of seasoning, some protein, and a few vegetables. We've included four ideas here to get you started, but feel free to personalize your soups with your favorite ingredients. Each makes one serving. Layer up!

KIMCHI MISO TOFU

380 calories

3 ounces soba noodles, cooked

1 teaspoon white miso paste, thinned with a little hot water

2 tablespoons Kimchi (page 67)

½ cup cubed firm tofu

COCONUT SHRIMP

391 calories

3½ ounces brown rice noodles, cooked

1 teaspoon Thai paste (page 64)

3 to 4 ounces shrimp, sautéed in a little coconut oil

1 small carrot, grated

Handful of alfalfa, radish, or broccoli sprouts

SHIITAKE SEAWEED MISO

178 calories

3 to 4 ounces soaked wakame

1 teaspoon white miso paste, thinned with a little hot water

2 or 3 dried shiitake mushrooms, soaked, drained, and sliced

½ cup cubed smoked tofu

CHICKEN AND BABY KALE LAKSA

370 calories

3 ounces soba noodles, cooked

1 teaspoon Laksa Paste (page 63)

½ cup shredded cooked chicken

2 to 3 ounces kale leaves or baby spinach

8

Beyond the Cleanse

We hope that our soup cleanses inspire you to include more soups in your day-to-day diet and help you to get into the habit of cooking easy, delicious, healthy recipes from scratch.

We are far from perfect ourselves, so we have to remind ourselves every now and then of a few simple principles for happy and healthy living. We always feel our best when we are in balance with ourselves and our bodies, which means exercising regularly (but never obsessively), eating natural foods, and enjoying life.

Tips for life beyond the cleanse

Healthy Eating

- After a cleanse, make an effort to keep your kitchen tidy and stocked with healthy ingredients. Always have a variety of grains (such as quinoa, buckwheat, barley, and rice) and lentils on hand to cook and plenty of spices and seeds for scattering over soups to add a bit of crunch.

- We usually have some tofu marinating in various spices and other seasonings in the fridge. We just open up the spice drawer and see what looks good: sumac and za'atar, nori flakes and sesame, or turmeric and cumin.

- Plan your meals for the week ahead, looking at what you already have and then adding your fresh ingredients. Batch cooking on Sunday is such a great way to set up a healthy week of eating, from soups for your lunches or a lovely stew that will keep you going early on in the week with different vegetables.

- Keep making stock, especially chicken and vegetable. It's the basis of so many great dishes, and you have delicious roast chicken to enjoy, too.

- Eat fresh fish at least once or twice a week. Cold-water oily fish such as salmon, mackerel, sardines, and anchovies are particularly good, as they are packed with healthy fats.

- Be adventurous while also knowing you can fall back on a growing list of healthy favorites. People often tell us that our Lemon Chicken and Mint soup (page 108) has become one of their household staples.

- Don't fall back into old habits of being on the computer or watching television while eating. Keep mealtimes for eating or for sharing.

- Keep your portion sizes modest, but satisfying.

- Drink plenty of water and your favorite herbal teas.

- Don't obsess about food. Don't feel guilty for having a slice of cake every now and then. Relax and enjoy it. It's amazing how well the digestive system responds in kind.

Healthy Living

- Always find ways to be as active as possible throughout the day. If you work in an office, for example, go for a walk at lunchtime or walk or bike some of the way to work and back home. Make a conscious effort to get up from your desk every couple of hours to stretch your legs and clear your mind.

- Find an exercise that you really enjoy. It might be a class once or twice a week such as kettlebells, Zumba, or spinning. You might love CrossFit, swimming, cycling, or running. If you love yoga or Pilates, go for it. There are so many choices nowadays that even if you didn't love sports when you were in school, there's probably an activity you'll enjoy.

- Start small when making changes. Use a fitness app. Add a couple of minutes each day, and before you know it, you'll be running 5k to 10k races or doing a difficult yoga pose. The same goes for creating any kind of healthy habit—long-term changes come from taking one small step at a time.

- Continue to take time out for yourself beyond a cleanse. Your mind and your body are incredible, so take care of them, whether through quiet contemplation in the morning or evening, booking a regular massage appointment, or meditating daily.

- Forgive us for sounding a little "woo woo," but for us gratitude is a big part of living healthily and in balance. The more we appreciate everything in our lives, the better we feel about ourselves and naturally want to take care of our bodies. Give thanks for something every day.

- Be curious about yourself, how you feel, and what you do every day to nourish your body, mind, and spirit.

Nutritional Information

CONDIMENTS

LAKSA PASTE
Per 3½ ounces: 170 calories; 3g protein; 12g total fat; 2g saturated fat; 16g carbohydrate; 3g fiber; 18mg sodium

THAI PASTE
Per 3½ ounces: 490 calories; 10g protein; 0g total fat; 120g carbohydrate; 20g fiber; 520mg sodium

UMAMI MUSTARD
Per 3½ ounces: 280 calories; 7g protein; 11g total fat; 1g saturated fat; 20g carbohydrate; 3.5g fiber; 140mg sodium

CLEANSE SPICE MIX
Per 3½ ounces: 249 calories; 20g protein; 20g total fat; 0g saturated fat; 20g carbohydrate; 20g fiber; 40mg sodium

CLEANSE DUKKAH
Per 3½ ounces: 340 calories; 16g protein; 28g total fat; 4g saturated fat; 8g carbohydrates; 6g fiber; 8mg sodium

KIMCHI
Per 3½ ounces: 42 calories; 2g protein; 0.2g fat; 7g carbohydrate; 3g fiber; 2810 mg sodium

SAFFRON YOGURT
Per 3½ ounces: 194 calories; 5g protein; 17g total fat; 7g saturated fat; 8g carbohydrate; 0g fiber; 91mg sodium

STOCKS AND BROTHS

ROAST CHICKEN AND BROWN STOCK
Per 1 quart: 130 calories; 16g protein; 5g total fat; 1g saturated fat; 4g carbohydrate; 5g fiber; 442mg sodium

SEAWEED BROTH
Per 1 quart: 49 calories; 2g protein; 1g total fat; 0.5g saturated fat; 8g carbohydrate; 2g fiber; 648mg sodium

TURMERIC, GINGER, AND LEMONGRASS BROTH
Per 1 quart: 30 calories; 1g protein; 0g fat; 8g carbohydrate; 1g fiber; 8mg sodium

BONE BROTH
Per 1 quart: 220 calories; 32g protein; 5g total fat; 1g saturated fat; 9g carbohydrate; 5g fiber; 169mg sodium

VEGETABLE STOCK
Per 1 quart: 78 calories; 1g protein; 1g fat; 0g saturated fat; 11g carbohydrate; 2g fiber; 368mg sodium

BREAKFAST

OVERNIGHT OATS
Per serving: 221 calories; 8g protein; 8g total fat; 2g saturated fat; 30g carbohydrate; 8g fiber; 114mg sodium

CLOVE-SPICED APPLE
Per serving: 165 calories; 2g protein; 8g total fat; 4g saturated fat; 26g carbohydrate; 5g fiber; 2mg sodium

BIRCHER
Per serving: 152 calories; 3g protein; 5g total fat; 1g saturated fat; 27g carbohydrate; 5g fiber; 2mg sodium

BERRY COMPOTE
Per serving: 59 calories; 0g protein; 0g fat; 14g carbohydrate; 1g fiber; 7mg sodium

EGG DROP SOUP WITH NORI
Per serving: 330 calories; 23g protein; 20g total fat; 5g saturated fat; 15g carbohydrate; 4g fiber; 1841mg sodium

MISO BREAKFAST BROTH
Per serving: 148 calories; 9g protein; 5g total fat; 1g saturated fat; 18g carbohydrate; 6g fiber; 274mg sodium

SMOOTHIES

BERRY KEFIR BOOSTER
Per serving: 146 calories; 6g protein; 2g total fat; 1g saturated fat; 28g carbohydrate; 4g fiber; 99mg sodium

ALMOND CHIA
Per serving: 312 calories; 8g protein; 18g total fat; 6g saturated fat; 32g carbohydrate; 8g fiber; 61mg sodium

AVOCADO NUTS
Per serving: 271 calories; 6g protein; 21g total fat; 2g saturated fat; 17g carbohydrate; 7g fiber; 231mg sodium

SNACKS

NOURISH BITES
Per serving: 150 calories; 3g protein; 10g total fat; 5g saturated fat; 13g carbohydrates; 3g fiber; 15mg sodium

KALE CRISPS
Per serving (the whole recipe): 225 calories; 7g protein; 20g total fat; 3g saturated fat; 10g carbohydrate; 4g fiber; 329mg sodium

TURMERIC AND BLACK PEPPER OATCAKES
Per serving: 51 calories; 1g protein; 2g total fat; 1g saturated fat; 8g carbohydrate; 1g fiber; 29mg sodium

SOUPS

RESOLVE

AVOCADO, LEMON, TURMERIC, AND CAYENNE
Per serving: 163 calories; 2g protein; 15g total fat; 9g saturated fat; 7g carbohydrate; 4g fiber; 290mg sodium

CORN, KALE, AND AVOCADO
Per serving: 230 calories; 7g protein; 17g total fat; 10g saturated fat; 18g carbohydrate; 13g fiber; 51mg sodium

BALTI-SPICED CAULIFLOWER
Per serving: 214 calories; 6g protein; 15g total fat; 2g saturated fat; 19g carbohydrate; 7g fiber; 80mg sodium

BEETS, COCONUT, AND SALMON
Per serving: 307 calories; 18g protein; 15g total fat; 12g saturated fat; 29g carbohydrates; 6g fiber; 219mg sodium

CHICKEN SOUP FOR THE CLEANSED SOUL
Per serving: 286 calories; 28g protein; 16g total fat; 3g saturated fat; 8g carbohydrate; 3g fiber; 241mg sodium

CURRIED PARSNIP AND APPLE
Per serving: 277 calories; 2g protein; 19g total fat; 11g saturated fat; 24g carbohydrate; 8g fiber; 52mg sodium

GREEN GAZPACHO
Per serving: 199 calories; 5g protein; 15g total fat; 3g saturated fat; 13g carbohydrates; 6g fiber; 30mg sodium

HOT CUCUMBER WITH SALMON
Per serving: 275 calories; 24g protein; 10g total fat; 3g saturated fat; 18g carbohydrate; 3g fiber; 802mg sodium

HOT CUCUMBER WITH BARLEY
Per serving: 206 calories; 6g protein; 3g total fat; 2g saturated fat; 37g carbohydrate; 7g fiber; 561mg sodium

LEEK, FENNEL, AND CELERY WITH RED LENTILS
Per serving: 237 calories; 11g protein; 8g total fat; 1g saturated fat; 32g carbohydrates; 12g fiber; 179mg sodium

SOUTH INDIAN MAHIMAHI WITH SEA BEANS
Per serving: 349 calories; 28g protein; 18g total fat; 13g saturated fat; 18g carbohydrates; 5g fiber; 596mg sodium

SALMON POACHED IN LEMONGRASS TEA
Per serving: 309 calories; 31g protein; 20g total fat; 5g saturated fat; 2g carbohydrate; 1g fiber; 115mg sodium

SUMMER CHICKEN
Per serving: 268 calories; 38g protein; 6g total fat; 3g saturated fat; 14g carbohydrate; 5g fiber; 37mg sodium

WILD GARLIC, BABY SPINACH, AND OLIVES
Per serving: 211 calories; 4g protein; 15g total fat; 2g saturated fat; 14g carbohydrate; 2g fiber; 450mg sodium

REDUCE AND REBALANCE

ASPARAGUS MIMOSA
Per serving: 241 calories; 14g protein; 14g total fat; 3g saturated fat; 15g carbohydrates; 3g fiber; 573mg sodium

CHICKEN AND ZUCCHINI THAI NOODLE SOUP
Per serving: 383 calories; 33g protein; 21g total fat; 16g saturated fat; 6g carbohydrate; 1g fiber; 170mg sodium

COCONUT CHICKEN WITH TURMERIC AND KALE
Per serving: 378 calories; 24g protein; 22g total fat; 13g saturated fat; 26g carbohydrate; 6g fiber; 108mg sodium

ZUCCHINI, LEMON, AND THYME
Per serving: 188 calories; 5g protein; 18g total fat; 3g saturated fat; 4g carbohydrate; 2g fiber; 17mg sodium

FIVE-SPICE TOFU
Per serving: 146 calories; 15g protein; 8g total fat; 1g saturated fat; 6g carbohydrate; 3g fiber; 426mg sodium

HARISSA CAULIFLOWER AND CORN
Per serving: 239 calories; 9g protein; 10g total fat; 1g saturated fat; 30g carbohydrates; 12g fiber; 158mg sodium

BUTTERNUT SQUASH AND HORSERADISH
Per serving: 239 calories; 6g protein; 20g total fat; 3g saturated fat; 32g carbohydrates; 7g fiber; 73mg sodium

KITCHARI
Per serving: 219 calories; 6g protein; 17g total fat; 13g saturated fat; 16g carbohydrate; 5g fiber; 14mg sodium

LEMON CHICKEN AND MINT
Per serving: 174 calories; 20g protein; 8g total fat; 2g saturated fat; 8g carbohydrate; 2g fiber; 126mg sodium

PEA AND PRESERVED LEMON
Per serving: 134 calories; 11g protein; 3g total fat; 1g saturated fat; 21g carbohydrate; 5g fiber; 550mg sodium

TOMATO AND LEMON SOUP WITH SALSA
Per serving: 133 calories; 2g protein; 8g total fat; 1g saturated fat; 13g carbohydrate; 4g fiber; 52mg sodium

SAFFRON BROTH WITH SHRIMP
Per serving: 133 calories; 24g protein; 1g total fat; 0.2g saturated fat; 6g carbohydrate; 3g fiber; 274mg sodium

SICHUAN PEPPERCORNS AND CHICKEN
Per serving: 268 calories; 21g protein; 15g total fat; 4g saturated fat; 8g carbohydrate; 4g fiber; 877mg sodium

SMOKED EGGPLANT AND KEFIR
Per serving: 135 calories; 4g protein; 8g total fat; 2g saturated fat; 13g carbohydrate; 4g fiber; 31mg sodium

HOT SMOKED MUSHROOM
Per serving: 100 calories; 4g protein; 8g total fat; 6g saturated fat; 6g carbohydrate; 2g fiber; 50mg sodium

SPINACH AND SPICED ONION
Per serving: 180 calories; 5g protein; 9g total fat; 6g saturated fat; 18g carbohydrate; 6g fiber; 87mg sodium

SPRING CHICKEN
Per serving: 302 calories; 35g protein; 13g total fat; 4g saturated fat; 7g carbohydrate; 3g fiber; 57mg sodium

TOFU SEAWEED MISO
Per serving: 340 calories; 19g protein; 24g total fat; 4g saturated fat; 13g carbohydrate; 8g fiber; 1008mg sodium

SMOKED TOFU, TOMATO, AND BROCCOLI
Per serving: 111 calories; 6g protein; 5g total fat; 1g saturated fat; 10g carbohydrates; 4g fiber; 134mg sodium

RESTORE

AUTUMN CHICKEN
Per serving: 266 calories; 33g protein; 12g total fat; 4g saturated fat; 3g carbohydrate; 2g fiber; 25mg sodium

BUCKWHEAT BROTH
Per serving: 295 calories; 11g protein; 9g total fat; 6g saturated fat; 45g carbohydrate; 8g fiber; 1216mg sodium

BUTTERNUT SQUASH AND SAGE
Per serving: 309 calories; 6g protein; 15g total fat; 2g saturated fat; 45g carbohydrate; 13g fiber; 39mg sodium

CARDAMOM COCONUT BARLEY
Per serving: 413 calories; 13g protein; 27g total fat; 19g saturated fat; 23g carbohydrate; 3g fiber; 116mg sodium

CARROT, CUMIN, AND MISO SOUP WITH GRAIN SALAD
Per serving: 179 calories; 3g protein; 8g total fat; 6g saturated fat; 27g carbohydrate; 8g fiber; 231mg sodium
For the salad:
Per serving: 115 calories; 5g protein; 1g total fat; 0g saturated fat; 22g carbohydrate; 4g fiber; 10mg sodium

CARROT, GINGER, AND TANGERINE
Per serving: 146 calories; 2g protein; 8g total fat; 1g saturated fat; 19g carbohydrate; 5g fiber; 186mg sodium

CELERY ROOT AND UMAMI MUSTARD
Per serving: 199 calories; 3g protein; 16g total fat; 2g saturated fat; 18g carbohydrate; 9g fiber; 186mg sodium

CHICKEN CONGEE
Per serving: 388 calories; 34g protein; 13g total fat; 3g saturated fat; 29g carbohydrate; 2g fiber; 1115mg sodium

CINNAMON PUMPKIN
Per serving: 116 calories; 2g protein; 7g total fat; 1g saturated fat; 9g carbohydrate; 4g fiber; 43mg sodium

COD LAKSA
Per serving: 258 calories; 34g protein; 10g total fat; 4g saturated fat; 13g carbohydrate; 2g fiber; 474mg sodium

CUMIN-ROASTED SWEET POTATO WITH ONION AND POMEGRANATE MOLASSES
Per serving: 295 calories; 3g protein; 15g total fat; 2g saturated fat; 38g carbohydrate; 3g fiber; 110mg sodium

GINGER CARROT WITH SPICED COCONUT YOGURT
Per serving: 384 calories; 6g protein; 24g total fat; 9g saturated fat; 36g carbohydrate; 11g fiber; 262mg sodium

JERUSALEM ARTICHOKE AND FENNEL
Per serving: 314 calories; 7g protein; 18g total fat; 2g saturated fat; 34g carbohydrate; 5g fiber; 67mg sodium

LENTILS, SEASONAL GREENS, AND GINGER-CARROT COLESLAW
Per serving: 343 calories; 18g protein; 13g total fat; 3g saturated fat; 29g carbohydrate; 10g fiber; 50mg sodium

MAGIC SOUP
Per serving: 343 calories; 19g protein; 12g total fat; 7g saturated fat; 41g carbohydrate; 16g fiber; 76mg sodium

ROASTED BUCKWHEAT WITH ACHARI SPICES AND EXOTIC MUSHROOMS
Per serving: 305 calories; 7g protein; 16g total fat; 8g saturated fat; 35g carbohydrate; 7g fiber; 93mg sodium

SPROUTED SOUP
Per serving: 245 calories; 7g protein; 16g total fat; 3g saturated fat; 19g carbohydrate; 5g fiber; 23mg sodium

WHITE KIMCHI
Per serving: 118 calories; 8g protein; 6g fat; 2g saturated fat; 3g carbohydrate; 2g fiber; 2800mg sodium

RENEW

BARLEY BONE BROTH
Per serving: 284 calories; 6g protein; 12g total fat; 2g saturated fat; 35g carbohydrate; 6g fiber; 87mg sodium

BEETS AND CARAWAY
Per serving: 136 calories; 6g protein; 1g total fat; 1g saturated fat; 24g carbohydrate; 5g fiber; 112 mg sodium

CAULIFLOWER, GARLIC, AND WALNUT CRUMB
Per serving: 256 calories; 9g protein; 12g total fat; 1g saturated fat; 32g carbohydrate; 11g fiber; 236mg sodium

CHICKEN AND NETTLE TOPS
Per serving: 274 calories; 44g protein; 5g total fat; 2g saturated fat; 11g carbohydrate; 3g fiber; 1939mg sodium

FENNEL-CRUSTED SALMON WITH GINGER CABBAGE
Per serving: 311 calories; 31g protein; 15g total fat; 4g saturated fat; 10g total carbohydrate; 3g fiber; 140mg sodium

HARISSA BROTH WITH EGGPLANT AND QUINOA
Per serving: 194 calories; 4g protein; 12g total fat; 2g saturated fat; 16g carbohydrate; 4g fiber; 276mg sodium

GREEN PHO
Per serving: 77 calories; 5g protein; 1g total fat; 0g saturated fat; 9g carbohydrate; 4g fiber; 106mg sodium

MUSSELS AND LEEK
Per serving: 372 calories; 32g protein; 13g total fat; 6g saturated fat; 25g carbohydrate; 3g fiber; 731mg sodium

RAW SOUP
Per serving: 194 calories; 4g protein; 12g total fat; 3g saturated fat; 11g carbohydrate; 6g fiber; 13mg sodium

RADISH, CRAB, AND TURMERIC CONGEE
Per serving: 316 calories; 19g protein; 13g total fat; 3g saturated fat; 28g carbohydrate; 1g fiber; 120mg sodium

RED LENTIL AND TAMARIND
Per serving: 204 calories; 8g protein; 3g total fat; 1g saturated fat; 35g carbohydrate; 8g fiber; 130mg sodium

ROAST CHICKPEA
Per serving: 188 calories; 1g protein; 1g total fat; 1g saturated fat; 13g carbohydrate; 2g fiber; 11mg sodium

SESAME CHICKEN
Per serving: 362 calories; 30g protein; 12g total fat; 3g saturated fat; 32g carbohydrate; 3g fiber; 85mg sodium

SOPA DI QUINOA
Per serving: 381 calories; 6g protein; 33g total fat; 5g saturated fat; 18g carbohydrate; 6g fiber; 102mg sodium

SQUASH AND ALMOND BUTTER
Per serving: 376 calories; 9g protein; 17g total fat; 2g saturated fat; 51g carbohydrate; 11g fiber; 19mg sodium

WATERCRESS, FLAX, AND TOFU
Per serving: 248 calories; 14g protein; 17g total fat; 3g saturated fat; 10g carbohydrate; 4g fiber; 347mg sodium

WILD RICE, EDAMAME, AND RAINBOW CHARD
Per serving: 165 calories; 7g protein; 4g fat; 1g saturated fat; 24g carbohydrate; 4g fiber; 235mg sodium

WINTER CHICKEN
Per serving: 336 calories; 36g protein; 18g total fat; 5g saturated fat; 5g carbohydrate; 2g fiber; 42mg sodium

SOUP JARS

KIMCHI MISO TOFU
Per serving: 380 calories; 16g protein; 5g total fat; 1g saturated fat; 66g carbohydrate; 5g fiber; 1271mg sodium

COCONUT SHRIMP
Per serving: 391 calories; 23g protein; 3g total fat; 1g saturated fat; 71g carbohydrate; 5g fiber; 670mg sodium

SHIITAKE SEAWEED MISO
Per serving: 178 calories; 13g protein; 6g total fat; 1g saturated fat; 21g carbohydrate; 18g fiber; 217mg sodium

CHICKEN AND BABY KALE LAKSA
Per serving: 370 calories; 29g protein; 3g total fat; 1g saturated fat; 38g carbohydrates; 2g fiber; 213mg sodium

Acknowledgments

Thank you for buying this book and for cooking our recipes—we hope you've enjoyed them!

Thank you to the team at Orion, especially Tamsin, Amanda, and Helen, and to Clare Hulton. Thanks also to Victoria Wells for her invaluable nutritional advice.

Thanks as ever to our friend and talented photographer Regula Ysewijn.

And to our mentors and teachers, without whom we'd never have been able to create so many soups!

Index

About the Authors

Nicole Pisani has worked as head chef at Yotam Ottolenghi's Soho restaurant NOPI and Anna Hansen's Modern Pantry in London. Her passion is creating healthy and vibrant dishes with interesting ingredients and spice combinations. Visit FoodForHappiness.co.uk.

Kate Adams is a health writer and the author of the *Flat Tummy Club Diet*. She lost thirty-five pounds by eating recipes from *Magic Soup*.